Evolutionary Parenting

David Marshak

Fairhaven Spiral Press
ISBN-13: 978-0692692561

CONTENTS

To be an Evolutionary means to reach out beyond the edges of what has already occurred, to see oneself as journeying into uncreated territory…[Today] Evolutionaries are part of a larger movement—a fledging, unstructured, diverse movement but one with great cultural promise and significance.

Carter Phipps, *Evolutionaries*

APPRECIATION

I want to express my gratitude to all of the people whose interviews appear in this book. Thank you for your willingness to share your lives with me and your trust in me to present your stories accompanied by accurate and appropriate commentary. I also want to thank a number of people who allowed me to interview them for this project and whose interviews do not appear in this final draft. From all of you, I learned much more about the ways in which consciousness can guide evolutionary parenting within the daily lives of families.

I want to thank the Seattle Waldorf School for helping me to find some of the families whose stories appear in this book.

I want to express my most profound gratitude to Sri Aurobindo, Rudolf Steiner, and Hazrat Inayat Khan for the guidance they have given me in my life's work—and to Sri Ramana Maharshi for telling me to go home and saving my life. *I was so dense, you had to tell me twice.*

Finally I want to thank everyone I know in the SelfDesign community—colleagues, learners, and friends—whose commitment to learning and to evolution has buoyed me as I finally have brought this book to completion.

1 FIVE INSIGHTS

I have five insights to share with you. Each one alone is significant. Weaving these five insights together will give you an inspired understanding of your child's or children's becoming—and profound and specific guidance about how you can help them grow up into the fullness of their gifts and a life of meaning, satisfaction, accomplishment, contribution, and self-realization.

1

You already know the *first insight.* Every conception and birth of a human being is a wedding of flesh and soul.

Citing extensive and detailed research, Jenny Wade explains, "Two distinct sources of consciousness exist before birth and during the perinatal period"[1] (a number of weeks immediately before and after birth). One is tied to the fetus' development of a physical brain, which shows measurable brain activity around the start of the third trimester of the pregnancy. This consciousness is infantile and primarily sensory. The other consciousness is mature and displays several characteristics of transcendence: "it is a distinct self but has little ego...it registers thoughts, feelings, and actions but is not comprised of, or very attached to, these...it operates in a receptive mode...it is fully mature and insightful."[2]

Flesh and soul. Wade notes that

> …at some point during the pregnancy or perinatal
> period, the transcendent source becomes "stuck" to its
> body…For the majority of people, this joining
> coincides with the period when measurable brain wave
> activity commences. By the second day after birth,
> the two sources of awareness are bound together.[3]

The flesh of the newborn is new and very much a beginning of the physical body's unfoldment. The soul is complete at birth.

Each soul has its own purpose. As Michael Meade explains, "Each soul harbors a sense of divine meaning within and expects a call that awakens it to a life aligned with an inner sense of purpose."[4]

Maria Montessori called this soul quality *horme*, "the vital force that is active within him (the child) and…guides his efforts toward their goal."[5]

Jean Houston calls this same quality the *entelechy*, the dynamic purpose that is coded within each person.

> Entelechy is all about the possibilities encoded in each of us. For
> example it is the entelechy of an acorn to be an oak tree…It is
> possible to call upon the entelechy principle within us in such a
> way that it becomes personal, friendly, and even helpful. This
> entelechy principle can be expressed symbolically as a god or a
> guide. We feel its presence as…inspiration or motivation…[6]

James Hillman also employs the acorn image: in the acorn of the infant is the oak of that person's potential unfoldment. "Each person bears a uniqueness that asks to be lived and that is already present before it can be lived[7]…The soul of each of us…has selected an image or pattern that we live on earth."[8]

You know this deep down in your being, even if you have not put this knowing into so many words before. Your soul has apprehended the soul of your child.

Take a few moments now—close your eyes, be still within, and allow yourself to feel this soul-to-soul connection with your child.

2

The **second insight** follows from the first. Since the soul in its fullness is present from before birth, your child's soul is expressing its knowing through the vehicle of the physical body from the beginning of life. Yes, the soul is constrained by the infant's physical, emotional, and mental limitations—but the will of the infant is manifest from the first day of life outside the womb (and sometimes before). *And the will of the child at every age and stage is the expression of the soul's intent.* Rudolf Steiner calls the soul "the inner teacher." He urges that parents see the child's will not as their opponent but as a source of wisdom about what the child needs in any moment, with which they can ally their parental efforts.

To follow the guidance of the soul, the child needs freedom. As Tsolagiu M. A. RuizRazo, a Cherokee elder, explains, "Since connections with the inner spirit come alive only in a state of freedom, let her have as much freedom as possible during this time."[9] But children, who are full in soul but immature in body, heart, and mind, also need protection and boundaries that are appropriate to their individual nature and level of unfoldment.

So, the **second insight** is that the primary work of soul-informed parenting is gaining the wisdom and emotional maturity to give your child as much freedom as possible to live out her inner teacher's guidance while providing your child with safety and individually-appropriate boundaries.

Fortunately this work is not about perfection. Parental errors in judgment are inevitable, as are emotional responses that are too strong or misdirected. *The key is that you continue to strive to give these qualities of freedom with appropriate boundaries to your child. If this is your goal, you will no doubt succeed in this sufficiently to provide your child with the gift of unfolding into her/his potentials.*

Close your eyes now and feel this pattern within your heart: freedom within appropriate limits, safe and supportive boundaries.

3

The **third insight** follows from the second. To work at giving your child freedom with safety, you will inevitably have to grow yourself—emotionally, intellectually, and spiritually. Even with all of the demands of parenting, family life, and economic well-being, the more that you choose to participate in activities that will help you to grow, the better you'll be able to give your child what his or her soul needs.

This is not an option or a luxury. As you likely already know, parenting is its own spiritual path. Either you choose to embrace its challenges with consciousness and intention and see it as an organic curriculum for working with your own limitations and healing your own wounding—or you will be stuck re-enacting your own wounds in your children's lives.

All of us as parents have said, "I would never say that to my child the way my mother/father said it to me." And we have all heard the voices of our parents rushing out from between our own lips. When we act in this manner, the key is not to chastise or punish ourselves—but to acknowledge the pattern, explore its roots, and seek to release or transform it.

Perfection in parenting is not attainable. But when we consciously choose to experience parenting as a spiritual path and seek to learn and grow ourselves on that path, we do. It's the intent and the effort that matter. One excellent guide for this journey is the book *Everyday Blessings: The Inner Work of Mindful Parenting* by Myla and Jon Kabat-Zinn (Hyperion, 1997).

Close your eyes, bring stillness within, and allow yourself to see or feel your own path of parenting now.

4

The *fourth insight* is that there is information available to you now about the trajectory through which human beings unfold and grow in childhood and youth. Yes, each child is unique in the most literal sense of that word. In concert with that uniqueness, the vast majority of children and youth unfold and grow through similar patterns of unfoldment, through similar trajectories of growth. But each individual grows in his or her own way, at his or her own rate.

Some of these patterns of human unfoldment and development have been charted by psychologists during the past century. A more holistic description of human unfoldment was articulated by three spiritual teachers—Rudolf Steiner, Aurobindo Ghose, and Inayat Khan—during the second decade of the 20th century. This holistic description includes body, heart, mind, and soul—and the complex relationships among these systems of the human being. You can learn more about this "common vision" of human unfoldment in Chapter Two.

5

The *fifth insight* is that the very best parenting that you can provide for your children will also make a significant contribution to the evolution of human consciousness.

Many people now understand that we human beings need to evolve or we may well perish from our own genius run amuck. For an increasing number of people, this perception is the new *myth* of our increasingly globalized world. *Evolution is not something happening out there, somewhere. We are an integral part of it. Our capacity for growth in consciousness is the leading edge of the evolutionary process on the planet right now.*

Myth is a funny word. In common usage it has come to mean a story that is fundamentally untrue, as in "that's just a myth, it's not real." But the deeper meaning of the word is a sacred narrative in the sense that it contributes to systems of thought and values, and that people attach religious or spiritual significance to it. So a myth is a story that human beings use to explain and give meaning to their lives.

For example, the myth of the "modern era," beginning with

the birth of modern science in 17th century Europe, is that the problems of human life can be solved through the development of science and technology. What we've seen in recent decades is the slow dissolution of this myth for many people in so-called developed societies. We have come to see that while science and technology continue to be the fruits of human genius that have provided us with enormous benefits, both materially and philosophically, science and technology cannot solve many key human problems, particularly problems that deal with values and ethics. In addition, new technologies always come with costs as well as benefits, particularly if we lack the foresight to see the whole system of a new technology's implementation.

The myth of science is still powerful in our times. But a new myth that is only beginning to emerge from its scientific womb is the myth of evolution. Charles Darwin and Alfred Russel Wallace both published writings that introduced biological evolution to modern societies in 1859. Early in the 20th century Rudolf Steiner, Aurobindo Ghose, and Inayat Khan placed the biological evolution of life within a larger context, explaining that biological evolution was one stream in a larger reality of spiritual evolution. Aurobindo in particular focused on the evolution of human beings as a key element in this process.

A few decades later Teilhard de Chardin and Jean Gebser also wrote about the evolution of human consciousness, in Gebser's terms, from archaic consciousness, to magical, to mythical, to mental, to integral. While Gebser came to his knowing mostly intuitively, in mid 20th century Clare Graves used the tools of social science to develop what has become known as the Spiral Dynamics model of the evolution of human consciousness. Graves' model was articulated and popularized by Don Beck and Chris Cowan and then Ken Wilber and Steve McIntosh in more recent years. It was based on data collected from a wide range of individuals from all over the world and added detail to Gebser's model with a somewhat different listing of stages: archaic, tribal/magical, warrior, traditional, modernist, post-modern, integral.[10]

We all move up and down the spiral of consciousness as we go through our daily lives, but each person has a central position, an anchor stance, a consciousness core at any given moment in her/his life. Since you are reading this book, it's most likely that your core consciousness is either post-modern or integral.

Someone with a traditional core consciousness would reject the insights in this book as heretical to her or his religious beliefs. Someone with a modernist core consciousness would be likely to view this book's claims as fantasy or delusion.

Steve McIntosh in the book *Integral Consciousness and the Future of Evolution* characterizes post-modern consciousness with the following qualities and values: egalitarian, compassionate and inclusive, worldcentric morality, personal growth of the whole person, ecological, celebration of the feminine, and renewed spiritual freedom and creativity.[11] Paul Ray and Sherry Anderson use the term "cultural creatives"[12] to identify post-modern consciousness, drawing on a large scale social science investigation to discover that about 25% of adults in the United States and Canada and a somewhat higher percentage in western Europe (Great Britain, France, Germany, Holland, Belgium, Denmark, Norway, Sweden, Finland) hold "cultural creative values." Ray and Anderson define these as follows: ecological sustainability beyond environmentalism; globalism; feminism, women's issues, relationships, and family; altruism, self-actualization, alternative health care, spirituality, and spiritual psychology; and well-developed social conscience and social optimism.

The next step up the evolutionary spiral is integral consciousness. McIntosh characterizes integral consciousness with the following qualities and values: compassion for and appreciation of all previous stages in the evolution of human consciousness, a sense of personal responsibility for the problems of the world, appreciation of the sometimes paradoxical qualities of truth, aspiration for the harmonization of science and religion, and seeing spirituality in evolution.[9]

Integral consciousness supports many of the same values as does post-modern consciousness. But one key difference is that while people whose core is post-modern consciousness often polarize off people whose core is traditional or modernist, viewing them as ignorant or foolish or corrupt, integral consciousness provides the awareness that every stage in the spiral of human evolution is necessary to our unfoldment—and that every stage offers both positive and negative qualities.

Consider "fundamentalist religion." Many people from a post-modern consciousness core react with hostility to fundamentalist religion and see its believers as people who are choosing not to use their reason. Yet in the evolution of human consciousness, traditional consciousness—what we now call fundamentalist religion—was an enormous evolutionary step upward in its origins. For the first time rulers with power over the ruled were constrained by laws; for the first time people began to have rights that were protected with power.

Post-modernists or cultural creatives also often polarize off modernist consciousness. They see everyday in their lives how materialism, an unconstrained search for new technological powers, and ecological irresponsibility seem to be as central to modernist consciousness as its immense capacity for invention. So they blame science and technology for these failings. Yet science and technology also have given us enormous values and powerful tools on which most cultural creatives rely in their daily lives: comfort, safety, longevity, food and shelter, transportation, communications technologies, entertainment, and so on.

The gift of integral consciousness is the capacity it offers to perceive and act in new ways in the world. McIntosh explains:

> Integral consciousness is a way of seeing things—a perspective that arises from a new understanding of how evolution really works. Not just biological evolution, but the evolution of human awareness and human history. Integral consciousness comes about as people use the insights of integral philosophy to recognize how values and worldviews have arisen in sequential stages throughout history, and how these stages of development are alive today within the mind of each person.[13]

When you read the previous paragraphs about spiral dynamics, do you experience a negative or hostile emotional response? It's not unusual for people whose core consciousness is post-modern to experience a resentment of hierarchy. We've often experienced hierarchy as hurtful or oppressive, because in our times hierarchies often manifest in those ways both from traditional and modern consciousness sources: for example, traditional religions, modernist schools, and "democratic" governments that fail to embody their ideals. One liberating quality of post-modern consciousness is its rejection of oppressive hierarchies and its insistence on both equality and equity.

But some hierarchies are not oppressive. They are just the way that the universe works. Biological evolution has a hierarchical quality in that each succeeding form is more complex than its predecessor. Multi-celled organisms are more complex than single-celled ones. Animals are more complex than plants. Homo sapiens is more complex than chickens.

This same progression of increasing complexity describes the evolution of human consciousness. It's not that people who have a more evolved core of consciousness are more valuable. Rather it is that they have more complexity of perception and conception, a greater capacity for understanding the many complex systems within which we live, and a larger range of choices about how they can act in their lives.

Perhaps the most creative gift of integral consciousness is that it gives people the capacity to perceive the whole system of any particular phenomenon or situation and to act from that perception in ways that focus on healing and improving, not on blaming or finding fault. This enlargement of capacity leads to a deepening of self knowledge and an enhancement of wisdom.

We have come to a time of crisis in the evolution of humanity. This is global warming/climate change. It is an enormously dangerous phenomenon, because it may disrupt and damage the life support systems of many or most of the life forms on the planet.

But it is also a perfectly framed evolutionary crisis in that it is global and universal in its potential impact—and only fools will seek to use their wealth and power personally to avoid its calamities (as some of the wealthy and powerful surely will). We know that evolution is often provoked by crisis, that crisis can be a catalyst to the development of next steps in evolutionary unfoldment. We may not have chosen consciously to create the crisis of global warming, but it is indisputably here and, most likely, of our own making. If we hope to mitigate its impacts and respond to these in creative and life-affirming ways, we will need as many people on the planet as possible acting from a core of integral consciousness.

We need to evolve as a species to survive and thrive. Because we are aware of the evolutionary process now, we can choose to participate consciously, with clear intent.

There are two paths open to us for evolutionary participation. One is our own psychological and spiritual growth work, what we do as adults to become more integral, to become more whole. Judith Blackstone explains, "Personal evolution is a growing communion with this fundamental, unified ground of life. It is literally an expansion of our personal consciousness in space."[14]

Personal evolution is a process of moving towards increased integration of one's parts. Blackstone continues,

> A person is integrated when there is optimal interaction
> between all vibratory levels of her or his organism. This means
> that, without adjustment, one is aware of one's entire being all
> at once. The lack of fragmentation between the various parts of
> ourselves is what is known as wholeness.[15]

Anyone who is aware of humanity's need to evolve surely must bring her or his will and talents to this personal work. But the means through which adults can evolve from post-modern to integral consciousness—and beyond—is not the focus of this book.

This book is about the second path, which may be even more important than the first. This is the path of parenting. "Basically we are each the vessel and the vehicle of the essential motion of evolution,"[16] Blackstone asserts. Each human being literally embodies the evolutionary potential of the species. *So every parent who knows this knows that her or his parenting can make a contribution to the evolution of humanity.*

This book describes how a number of parents have begun this

work in recent years. You'll hear directly from these parents about their lives, their challenges and struggles and their accomplishments and satisfactions, their hardships and their joys. You'll also hear from a number of their young adult children who have been nurtured by the inspiration of evolutionary parenting.

Evolutionary parenting opens the door so children and teens, guided by their inner teachers and nurtured by their parents, can unfold toward their fullness of potential. The young adults you'll meet in this book all have accessed post-modern consciousness in their teens, and several have already moved on into integral consciousness.

Close your eyes now, still your body, and bring this phrase— evolutionary parenting—into your awareness. Let yourself sit with these words for a bit and see what comes up into your awareness.

Notes

1. Jenny Wade (1996). *Changes of Mind: A Holonomic Theory of the Evolution of Consciousness.* Albany, NY: State University of New York Press. Page 58.
2. Ibid. Page 54.
3. Ibid. Page 53.
4. Michael Meade (2008). *The World behind the World: Living at the Ends of Time.* Seattle: Greenfire Press. Pages 6-7.
5. Maria Montessori (1995). *The Absorbent Mind.* New York: Henry Holt and Co. Page 83.
6. Jean Houston (1992). *The Hero and the Goddess: The Odyssey As Mystery And Initiation.* New York: Ballantine Books. Page 62.
7. James Hillman (1996). *The Soul's Code: In Search of Character and Calling.* New York: Random House. Page 6.
8. Ibid. Page 8.
9. Tsolagiu M. A. RuizRazo (2004). *Tomorrow's Children: A Cherokee Elder's Guide To Parenting.* New Tazewell, TN: World Edition USA. Page 75.
10. These are the terms employed by Steve McIntosh in *Integral Consciousness and the Future of Evolution* (St. Paul, MN: Paragon House, 2007). Don Beck and Christopher Cowan

use the following terms for the same progression of stages of consciousness in *Spiral Dynamics: Mastering Values, Leadership, and Change : Exploring the New Science of Memetics* (Boston: Blackwell Publishers, 1996):

> Archaic-instinctive—survivalistic, automatic, reflexive
> Animistic-tribalistic magical-animistic
> Egocentric-exploitive power gods/dominionist
> Absolutistic-obedience mythic order—purposeful, authoritarian
> Multiplistic-achievist scientific/strategic
> Relativistic-personalistic—communitarian/egalitarian
> Systemic-integrative

11. Steve McIntosh (2007). *Integral Consciousness and the Future of Evolution* (St. Paul, MN: Paragon House, 2007. Page 56.
12. Paul Ray and Sherry Anderson (2000). *The Cultural Creatives. How 50 Million People Are Changing the World.* New York: Harmony Books.
13. Op cit. McIntosh. Page 84.
14. Judith Blackstone (1991). *The Subtle Self: Personal Growth and Spiritual Practice.* Berkeley, CA: North Atlantic Books. Page 59.
15. Ibid. Pages 56-57.
16. Ibid. Page 39.

2 THE PATH OF HUMAN UNFOLDMENT

Early in the 20th century James Mark Baldwin, an early American experimental psychologist and philosopher, may have been the first scientist to articulate the becoming of human beings in childhood and youth as a passage through varied and unique cognitive stages. In the late 1920s and 1930s, Jean Piaget, probably with influence from Baldwin's work, presented the first scientific description of the cognitive development of children and teens as a series of discrete stages. Piaget explained that the development of children was not a process of simple, linear growth but a movement through stages that were profoundly different, as summarized below.

Piaget's Stages of Cognitive Development

Sensorimotor (0-2 years) The child learns by doing: looking, touching, sucking. The child also has a primitive understanding of cause-and-effect relationships.

Object permanence appears around 9 months.

Preoperational (2-7 years) The child uses language and symbols, including letters and numbers. Egocentrism is also evident. Conservation marks the end of the preoperational stage and the beginning of concrete operations.

Concrete Operations (7-11/13) The child demonstrates conservation, reversibility, serial ordering, and a mature understanding of cause-and-effect relationships. Thinking at this stage is still concrete.

Formal Operations (12-14+) The individual demonstrates abstract thinking, including logic, deductive reasoning, comparison, and classification.

Since Piaget's discoveries gained prominence in the English-speaking world in the 1960s, thousands of developmental psychologists have conducted research that has confirmed and further detailed his findings. Yet more than a decade before Jean Piaget began his research, Maria Montessori in 1909 articulated a model of human development that included most of Piaget's insights and extended beyond them. Unlike Piaget whose initial research was focused primarily on his own children, Montessori observed children from many different families in a school that she started and led. While she was careful to identify herself as a scientist, Montessori also drew on her intuition for access to knowledge about children's development.

Montessori's model of human development focused on physical and intellectual development and extended beyond Piaget's descriptions into the specific processes of children's learning. At exactly the same moment in human evolutionary history—1910 to 1920—three men who were primarily spiritual teachers each independently articulated a model of human development that included Montessori's model and expanded it to include the whole human being. These three men were Rudolf Steiner, Aurobindo Ghose, and Inayat Khan, and their *common vision* of human development included the physical and the intellectual, the emotional and the spiritual, and the complex and intimate relationships among these four aspects of each human being. These three men also used the term *unfoldment* rather than *development* to indicate that the growth of the child was not only a progression of increasing complexity but also an ongoing, outer expression of inner potentials.

Steiner was a multi-faceted genius who made profound

contributions not only to our understanding of human unfoldment and education but also to our knowledge about organic farming, architecture, and the spiritual domain of human life. Ghose was an east Indian who first worked for Indian independence from England and then became a renowned mystic and spiritual teacher, both in India and in the West. Khan was also an east Indian who became the first Sufi master to teach in the United States and Europe. In an era when communication and transportation technologies had not yet brought the many lands of this planet into their present proximity, each of these three men had a profound understanding of the cultures of both the West and the East. Each of them carried elements of Western and Eastern traditions into his teachings and joined these elements with his own personal knowing to create a vision that was both a synthesis of East and West and the expression of his own spiritual intuition. (See Appendix One for more information about these three men.)

During the past two centuries, many spiritual teachers have talked and written about the nature of human beings. But only Inayat Khan, Rudolf Steiner, and Aurobindo Ghose have informed this discussion with detailed descriptions of both the process of human becoming in childhood and youth and the desired functions of child raising and education to support each child's and teen's unfoldment. These three men lived at the same historic moment, yet as far we know, they never met. Each one came to essentially the same vision of human unfoldment, this *common vision*, through his own spiritual intuition.

Each man described our evolutionary potential in the same way: one key vehicle for the ongoing evolution of our species is the extent to which the parenting and education that young people receive allows and nurtures each child's and teen's unfoldment toward her or his potential. The more this happens, the more our species will evolve in consciousness.

A Common Vision Of Human Nature

According to Steiner, Aurobindo, and Inayat Khan, the most fundamental nature of human beings is that we are complex systems of energy that include several interpenetrated and interrelated sub-systems. One—and only one—of these sub-systems consists of energy in the form of matter. The others are purely energetic. Each sub-system exists largely but not exclusively on a different plane of being. The various planes of being are simultaneously separate and integral and range from the lowest plane, matter, to the highest plane, spirit. Each human sub-system is connected to and affected by every other sub-system. Thus, we are profoundly interdependent among all of our parts and with all other energies with which we interact.

The four sub-systems are:

A physical being that exists on the material plane. This being is the body of matter. It includes the vehicles of the five physical senses, the breathing and circulation systems, the digestive organs, and the trunk and limbs. The physical body also includes the body consciousness, the awareness that emerges purely from the physical body.

A life-force being that exists on the next higher plane, the plane of life-force or vital energies. The life-force being exists on a plane of subtle energy that is of a higher and finer vibration than matter. This being consists of subtle energy that animates matter into the form of life. In the course of evolution, the life-force energy first manifested in plants, then in animals, and then in humans. It is part of what connects us with all other forms of life.

A mind or mental being that exists on the next higher plane. The mental being operates on the next higher plane of being and includes the memory; the element of mind that receives sensory data and translates these data into thought forms; the element of mind that apprehends vibrations from higher planes and translates them into images; and the intellect, the seat of reason.

A spiritual being that exists on still higher planes. Each person includes two levels of spiritual being: a personal spiritual quality, often called the *soul*, and a connection to the divine/absolute/universal, sometimes called the *spirit*. These levels of spiritual being embody the divine energy within the human person. It is this spiritual being that motivates personal unfoldment and the evolution of the individual—and, through the unfoldment of individuals, the evolution of the species.

In addition, both Aurobindo and Inayat Khan describe the ego as the false sense of self-created in early childhood when the spiritual self identifies with the physical, life-force, and mental beings. The ego is illusory and distorted in relation to the spiritual being, yet it is a necessary step in the unfoldment of the person. The ego is required for survival until the spiritual being can unfold and establish itself within the consciousness.

Aurobindo and Inayat Khan note that humans are transitional beings within the evolutionary process like all others before us: when we have fulfilled our potential, the next level of beings will emerge from us and continue to evolve.

A Common Vision Of Human Unfoldment: Birth To Age Twenty-One

In the broad outlines of their visions of human becoming from birth through age twenty-one, Rudolf Steiner, Aurobindo Ghose, and Inayat Khan share an even greater agreement than they do in their descriptions of human nature. While each spiritual teacher brings a distinct flavor to his descriptions, the details of these visions coincide to the extent that there are only a few important points of disagreement among them. Even these are more differences in emphasis than any sort of direct contradictions.

Their common vision of human becoming from birth through age twenty-one includes these elements:

The process of human becoming from birth through age twenty-one is an unfoldment of inherent potentials that require proper nurture if the young person's nature is to evolve to the extent of its capacities. Thus, what is central in determining the becoming of the young person is her nature **and** her nurture in relationship to each other.

Each child and youth is an organismic whole who contains within herself her own innate wisdom and motive force, her own *inner teacher*, to guide and power her unfoldment. The inner teacher is an expression of the soul. This wisdom and motive force direct the child to unfold in a direction and at a pace that are appropriate for her development, if he is allowed by adults to be guided by her inner teacher.

The unfoldment of the child and youth follows a course that is relatively consistent, regular, and foreseeable in its large outlines. Yet each individual unfolds at his own pace, which results in wide variations in the particular age when any given child experiences any particular step in his unfoldment. This process of unfoldment includes three major eras, each of about 6-8 years in length:

a. Birth through 6-7 years of age

b. 6-7 through 12–14 years of age

c. 12–14 through 21 years of age

As the child unfolds and grows, the evolution of his or her individual consciousness recapitulates the evolution of homo sapiens consciousness throughout its evolutionary history so far, as described by the spiral dynamics model: from archaic to tribal/magical, to warrior, to traditional, and, with the necessary nurturance and social and cultural opportunity, to modernist, post-modern, and integral.

At each stage or level of the unfoldment of consciousness, the child or youth first grows up into that new level and then identifies herself with it. Indeed this new quality of consciousness becomes her reality. There is nothing to be gained—and much may be lost— when adults try to rush a child or youth into the next stage before her inner teacher signals the proper time for the next movement upward. *Each era or stage in the unfoldment of the child and youth must be lived fully.* The principle that guides human growth is not haste or acceleration but the completeness of the unfoldment of the individual's potentials in each era of her life.

When the child or youth has lived a stage fully, he begins to access the next, higher stage and to disidentify with the previous stage. With a successful upward movement he transcends the previous stage, identifies with the higher stage, and includes positive elements of the previous stage in her consciousness. Thus the movement of unfolding is transcend and include.

What follows, drawn in broad strokes, is the common vision of human becoming between birth and age twenty-one described by Steiner, Aurobindo, and Inayat Khan.

The First Era: Birth Through 6 Years

In the first era, the child needs to direct her own activity as much as possible. She knows her experience as play, which is purposive to her. While her activity is more rewarding in its process than in its outcome, she needs the opportunity to experience a sense of completion about whatever she begins when she seeks such closure. She also needs to learn to satisfy her own needs as is appropriate to her age. The child who is free to direct her own activity will inevitably act in this way, for her inner wisdom will lead her to choose activities that meet her immediate growth needs.

In these years the child learns primarily by imitation. She perceives whatever is in her environment, including its physical, emotional, moral, mental, and spiritual aspects, and imitates these examples. As she learns through imitation, she does not gain from being taught rules or abstractions. What serves her unfoldment best is the provision of good examples that she can imitate: adults who are engaged in their own ongoing growth and who manifest truth-making, order, and spiritual opening as well as a calm and patient consistency in their behavior toward the child.

The young child also needs love, affection, support, and a high quality of care. When the child receives such nurturance, she experiences an interwoven happiness and trust and gains confidence in the fundamental goodness of life. This confidence evokes an inner joy and relaxation that provide her with even more nurturance.

The child needs to experience awe and reverence and to learn a feeling of gratitude toward the spiritual world for the wonders of the universe. She can best gain these experiences by participating with adults in rituals that evoke these feelings in the adults. The child will then learn them through her imitation of the adults' emotional and spiritual experience.

The first part of this era extends through the first two and half years of the child's life, when she belongs in the family. Each of these years has a powerful effect on the child's becoming, but all three teachers stress the critical importance of the first year in particular. While Aurobindo and Steiner describe the significance of the examples the child has in this year, Inayat Khan details the mechanism through which these examples influence the infant. At birth, Khan explains, the infant's soul, her spiritual being, is unfinished. The impressions that the child receives in her first year from her parents influence the completion of her spiritual being, either for the good or not.

In these years the child's primary growth tasks include learning to crawl, to stand and walk, and to speak and think. All of these tasks involve the exercise of her will, which must be allowed as much expression as possible without restriction from adults. The more the child can express her will in these years, Inayat Khan, Aurobindo, and Steiner strongly agree, the more powerful and spiritually open she will be later on.

Both Steiner and Inayat Khan note that the child's cutting of her first teeth is the outward manifestation of the initial unfoldment of her thinking.

In her third year the child first gains a sense of herself as a separate person, when what Aurobindo and Inayat Khan call the ego, the false sense of self, develops. Once her ego has evolved into consciousness, the child moves into the second part of this era, from about two and a half years of age into her seventh year.

In these years the child needs to experience what Inayat Khan calls "kingship": the freedom to follow her own initiative within safe boundaries, and, as much as possible, the absence of worry, anxiety, competition, and ambition. While the child benefits from experiencing social contexts beyond the family part of the time, she needs such contexts to be as free of competition and conflict as possible.

Steiner and Inayat Khan both specifically note the child's need for environments that allow unchecked movement and initiative, that encourage the child's fancy and imagination. She needs not to be directed to the learning of numbers or language but to be allowed to play according to her own inclination. The child's play is the expression of her spiritual being. The more he is allowed to express her spiritual being freely, the more he can evolve spiritually as he unfolds. The more she is directed into the learning of symbols in these years, the shallower and more materialistic she will become in later life.

The child also needs environments and playthings that are incomplete and open-ended. Such environments and toys require her to engage her imagination in completing them.

The child continues to learn primarily through the imitation of adults. She needs warmth and cheerfulness from adults as well as positive moral and spiritual examples. She also needs to learn from the example of nature, to be immersed in the rhythms and beauties of the natural world. In experiencing nature in this way, the child can discover another path that leads to awe, reverence, and gratitude. The more that the adults who guide her also experience these feelings in their own relationship with the natural world, the more the child will be open to learning from their example.

The Second Era: 6 Through 12–14 Years

In her seventh year the child begins to move from the first era into the second. While he still lives within an ongoing stream of inner images and memories that are beyond his control, as part of this transition the child often experiences a diminution of his will. Such an inner experience is confusing to the child. Before, he usually knew what he wanted to do; now he is sometimes lost, without motivation. This transformation often leads to inner conflict, expressed as restlessness or obstinacy. Only with his evolution into the second era of life can the child move through this conflict and confusion and enter a new quality of experience. Steiner marks the beginning of the second era with the changing of the teeth, which is both a signal of and an element in the process of transformation.

Aurobindo describes this transformation as the opening of the psychic being, the soul. Steiner also teaches that this second era is primarily focused on the growth of the soul. Inayat Khan explains that with the beginning of this era, the child's inner conflict dissipates, and he grows calmer and more harmonious. In this era the child learns best through joyous aesthetic activity: drawing, painting, music, dancing, movement, and so on. These years are a time when the child experiences compelling inner rhythms that he can best express through the arts. Yet the child does not benefit from any kind of artistic training now. Rather, what he needs is the opportunity for free expression of his own initiative through color, shape, pattern, music, and rhythm. This initiative flows from his spiritual being. When it is manifested through aesthetic activity, its expression helps the spiritual being to evolve. The child also needs to experience a regular rhythm in the course of his daily life.

With the growth of the adult teeth, the child begins to think, though in a very concrete manner, because his thinking is still fused with his physical body. It comes alive as a largely imageic process that is strongly influenced by his emotions. The child also begins to unfold a capacity for moral understanding.

Now the child needs to learn to write and read his native language and to gain competence in the initial understandings and skills of mathematics. Yet in this learning, too, he can be most fully engaged through the use of rhythm as a method of teaching.

As the child learns through his senses, feelings, and imagination in these years, he needs to be spared from theories and other abstractions that have little meaning for his. Instead he needs to experience stories and pictures that convey aesthetic and moral values, that he can visualize and take within himself for guidance and enduring meaning. He has the capacity to learn profoundly from stories of great and wonderful personalities from myth and history. Such stories evoke inner imagery, grounded in feelings of reverence and veneration, and arouse a spirit of emulation in the child's spiritual being that aids the growth of his character and moral nature.

Steiner teaches that the child's most powerful learning in these years results from his "discipleship" to an adult: a teacher by necessity of what that role demands, not a parent. In this experience of "discipleship," the child can revere and emulate this teacher. From this relationship he can also learn about the bounds of natural authority. Both Aurobindo and Inayat Khan note that the child needs to experience teachers who embody integrity and nobility of character. But they do not mention the kind of intense relationship with a single adult to which Steiner gives so much significance.

In this era the child needs to learn good habits and attitudes, particularly patience, endurance, and perseverance. He needs to be encouraged to wait when necessary and to bring what he begins to completion. He also needs to continue to develop his relationship with nature, as his direct experience of nature supports his intellectual and spiritual unfoldment.

By the time the child has entered this second era, he has lost the clarity of will that directed his younger activity. He rejects imitation as "babyish" and often seeks guidance from adults.

In the first three years of this era, the child needs to build on the gratitude to the spiritual world that was evoked within his in the preceding years in two ways. He needs to learn the will to love: first feeling this caring for a revered adult(s), then expanding its range to others and to nature. He also needs to learn his first ideals: respect for elders and the joy that flows from giving respect; self-respect; a sense of duty; and his first feeling of the divine ideal. During these years the child can connect his feelings of reverence for the natural world with his ideal of the divine, bringing feeling to that ideal and expressing it as his first experiences of worship.

The child's feeling for rhythm and his need to experience the world through rhythm are most intense in these first years of the second era. His awarenesses are sensual and imaginative. He wants to interact with that which is alive, plants and animals, and that which is full of life, stories and pictures.

In these years the child is also engaged in grounding himself: developing a sense of his place in the family, school, and peer group. Finally the child's memory awakens with the changing of the teeth and needs to be cultivated on a regular basis through rhythms of movement, tables, and rhymes.

At nine years of age, the child may experience an intense yet unformulated and unarticulated questioning of his respect and reverence for his elders. He needs adults to respond to this questioning not with fear or anger but with openness and love. At this time the child may also experience a new intensity in his social needs, seeking to be with his peers more and placing more import in their acceptance of his.

At ten years of age, the child enters the second part of this era. He begins to differentiate himself more profoundly from the world around his and to take on patterns of individuality that will be with his for the rest of his life. In this eleventh year of his life and through the remaining years of this era, he begins to discover what his strengths and proclivities are. He also has the potential to begin to discover his calling.

The child is very much open to knowledge in these years. He still can learn from stories of heroes and heroines, though the learning now takes place on a more complex level. He also begins to develop powers of concentration and needs to practice them through artistic and craft activities that require attention, patience, and coordination.

At eleven years of age, the child is ready to learn about cause and effect. Prior to this age, the less he interacts with this kind of reasoning, the richer the life of his spiritual being will be. Now he is ready to use his reason to observe cause and effect in the natural world and explore the relationships between them. He can also learn to classify, define, and discriminate what he perceives in nature.

At this age the child can extend his feeling for the divine and open to spiritual experience for the first time. His feelings of wonder and awe for nature can take his beyond the boundaries of his physical being and bring his to a visceral awareness of the divine ideal both beyond and within himself. This kind of experience is an opening to the reality of spirit, though not the spiritual awakening to which he can come at the end of his youth. It is both a felt experience and a validation of spirit—and an intimation of his potential for a more complete awakening later on.

In the last year or two of this era, the child's limbs and trunk begin to grow quickly. His muscles enlarge and strengthen. He begins to develop an awareness of her sexual identity. What he needs now is not to be rushed into the world of adolescence but to be allowed to continue to unfold at her own pace.

The Third Era: 12–14 Through 21 Years

The third era of childhood and youth begins with the onset of puberty and continues at least until age twenty-one. It is marked by dramatic growth and change in the physical body, which is the material aspect of a much larger transformation.

As this era begins, the youth starts to develop a more complete reason, which is dominated by independent, critical thought and the ability to work with abstraction. Her thinking is now based within her mind, not her emotion. She examines what lies around her with her growing but still inconsistent reason. She no longer accepts authority on its own terms but evaluates its validity, often choosing to question and challenge it.

The youth's inner life is vastly expanded as her thinking evolves. Both her new mode of thinking and her maturing feeling lead her to an increasingly larger awareness of herself and the world. As her inner life grows, the youth finds passion and delight in her ideas, much as the younger child experiences these feelings in her interaction with pictures and stories.

In these years the youth manifests her sexual characteristics and opens to sexuality and personal love. She also can experience the spiritual counterpart of personal love: a powerful caring for all living things expressed as an idealism bound up in imagination. As she learns about her own idealism, the youth both seeks people who share her values and continues to consider and explore her ideals to test their value to her as guides for her behavior.

The youth often experiences the third era, and particularly its first third, as a time of intense turmoil, struggle, inner conflict, and temporary regressions. She gains the beginnings of adult comprehension and maturity but manifests these inconsistently. At times she is clear and responsible, at other times absent-minded, moody, self-absorbed, and oblivious of others.

What the youth needs in these years is to explore both

within—her feelings, passions, intuitions, thoughts, and questions—and without—her ideas and experiences and the people with whom he interacts. She needs the freedom to consider and think on her own, make her own decisions, experience their consequences, and learn from them. She also needs the help and support of adults who understand her inconstancy but who nonetheless respect her integrity and the demands of her unfoldment. The youth needs neither criticism nor repression from adults but support and appreciation of her positive qualities. She needs a consistent balance: firm and constant support and supervision, with gradually increasing freedom and responsibility. The young person responds positively to adult leadership that respects her. The youth also needs the experience of adventure: to explore beyond the world of family and school and to gain new learnings and new relationships.

The third era is naturally a time of self-absorption. In response to this tendency, the youth needs to be helped gently to think and feel beyond herself. He needs to learn about how things work in the practical world and to discover the contributions that previous generations have made to her culture. As she experiences this learning about the past, she needs to be engaged in imagining what her generation can do to make the world a better place. The youth also needs to cultivate a receptive, in-taking attitude and to practice this regularly for short times to counter her natural imbalance between expression and receptivity.

In the first third of this era, the youth experiences an intense inconsistency over which she has little control. In the middle third, she begins to develop a center and needs to seek balance and increasing self-control. From fifteen years of age on, her major growth task is the development of her will, for it is the will that will direct and power her later spiritual awakening. She can work toward the unfoldment of her will through the practice of concentration and other will-related tasks.

In the final third of this era, the youth gains self-possession and clarity and finally becomes more of an adult than a child. In her twenty-first year, the young adult has the capacity to awaken to a conscious awareness of her spiritual being. This awakening brings her to an experience of the divine spirit within herself.

Joseph Chilton Pearce adds a significant insight to the common vision's portrait of adolescence. Pearce explains that teens often experience three felt qualities that most adults in their lives fail to understand and honor. The first is an energetic idealism, often raw and exaggerated but nonetheless true in its core nature. Teens begin to see the limitations and failures of adults and envision the possibility of rectifying the failures and improving on the limitations. This idealism may seem unrealistic to adults, but within the current context of accelerating evolutionary change in human culture, who can claim that they know for certain what's realistic and what is not?

Second, many or most teens experience a feeling of great expectations for their own lives. For most this is a barely conscious recognition that we each have the capacity to experience a calling in our lives and that a calling is the expression of the will, which is the expression of the soul. Even teens who have had very restricted or repressed lives in childhood can open to a sort of transparency in adolescence during which they gain some felt sense of their souls. Teens experience their souls as an attraction, a strong curiosity, a pull in a particular direction in life, or a clearly articulated calling.

Third, many or most teens experience a feeling of what Pearce calls "hidden greatness." While adolescents are prone to self-centeredness or narcissism as a regular part of their unfoldment, this feeling of "hidden greatness" is something different. It's another way that the soul can come into the consciousness of the teen, sometimes as a whisper and other times as a shout. And it can be a feeling of wholeness—or of the potential for wholeness. This feeling of "hidden greatness" presages the potential of the teen to access integral consciousness and to open fully to soul and spirit in early adulthood so she can claim her own calling, her life purpose.

In terms of the spiral dynamics model, the common vision tells us that teens can fully experience modernist consciousness in adolescence, then evolve upwards to post-modern consciousness, and then begin to access integral consciousness by the end of this third era in their lives.

When we consider adolescence in the context of evolution, we know first that our sub-species, Homo sapiens sapiens, evolved from archaic Homo sapiens about 200,000 years ago; the oldest fossil record of anatomically modern humans are the Omo remains that date to 195,000 years ago. We reached full "behavioral modernity" around 50,000 years ago. *However, adolescence as we know it today was first conceptualized only a little more than 100 years ago.* For almost all of our tens of thousands of years as a sub-species, humans became adults once they reached puberty. Teenagers lived as adults, worked as adults, had children, and took on all of the responsibilities of adults.

G. Stanley Hall was the first to name adolescence—from the Latin *adolescere,* meaning "to grow up"—in his 1904 book, *Adolescence: Its Psychology and Its Relations to Physiology, Anthropology, Sociology, Sex, Crime, Religion, and Education.* Yet the first significant adolescent population did not appear in the United States until the post-World War II baby boomers began to enter their teens in the late 1950s. In 1900 barely 10 percent of the 14-17 year olds were enrolled in school, the key social marker of a time-out between childhood and adulthood. During the next five decades school enrollment in this age group exploded from the atypical to the norm: to 31 percent in the 1920, 50 percent in 1930, 73 percent in 1940, 76 percent in 1950, and 87 percent in 1960. During these decades adolescence evolved from an uncommon experience available mainly to children of the wealthy to the normative cultural experience for teens in the United States. Other industrial, modernist nations have followed a similar trajectory of change.

The key insight in this data is this: *within our long history as a sub-species, adolescence is a startlingly new phenomenon*—and it's not surprising at all that we don't know that much about its potentials.

What the common vision tells us is that adolescence is likely the key to the next steps in human evolution.

What did adults do with these tens of millions of adolescents when they first appeared without warning? They sentenced them to 30+ hours each week in secondary schools plus more hours for homework, even though the paradigm of the academic high school had been created for a very different purpose and a much smaller fraction of the population. Adults excluded teens from most of adult life and, instead, dumped them into the age ghetto that quickly became youth culture.

It's not at all surprising that our initial social and cultural responses to the sudden appearance of tens of millions of adolescents were so misguided. The manifestation of adolescence on a mass scale was a radically new evolutionary step for homo sapiens. For the first time in our existence as a species, we had an opportunity for tens of millions of individual humans to explore and develop their human potential, to find their gifts and their callings, and to evolve into a much more complex and articulated consciousness. Right on schedule, the human potential movement—part psychology, part spirituality—emerged in the 1960's culture and began developing tools for this evolutionary step upward. At the very same time, spiritual teachers from Asia came to North America and western Europe in some numbers and began to teach the tools for evolving consciousness that are embedded in most Asian spiritual traditions.

But the men with power—and they were almost all men—in our industrial society had no insight into either evolution or human development. They feared the human potential movement and ridiculed Asian spiritual traditions, and they fought to delegitimize these insights and destroy this initial evolutionary flowering. They worked hard in this campaign—and they are still working harder than ever—to keep adolescents in conventional, industrial paradigm schools, youth culture ghettos, which block both the development and maturation of individuals and the evolution of the species. *Every political and educational leader who wants every teen to learn the same material at the same time as every other teen is an obstacle to the evolution of our species that our times demand.*

So here we are now, three generations into adolescence, and as a culture we are ignoring or repressing this profound evolutionary possibility.

Margaret Mead explained one aspect of where we need to go

with adolescence in terms of cultural evolution in her book, *Culture and Commitment*.[1] Mead describes three cultural paradigms in terms of their teaching/learning relationships between the young and the old:

- *postfigurative*, in which children learn primarily from their parents and other adults

- *cofigurative*, in which both children and adults learn primarily from their peers, and

- *prefigurative*, in which children learn from their parents, other adults, and each other, and adults learn from their children and other members of their children's generation.

All human societies prior to the 20th century were *postfigurative*. Pre-agricultural societies, in which humans lived for 80%-95% of our species life, changed little if any. Agricultural societies, beginning about 10.000 years ago, did change but slowly enough not to alter the dynamics of cultural transmission. In contrast industrial societies have experienced continually accelerating change for about 250 years, a moment in the history of the species.

What our societal leaders unknowingly did in the 1950s in the United States, Canada, and western Europe was to create a *cofigurative* culture. Adolescents were sentenced to years of schooling, even though formal schooling is unengaging and unproductive for most of them. They were excluded from meaningful roles in the adult world, and teens' capacity for perceiving the present in a quickly changing society more acutely than their parents was ignored or ridiculed. Adolescents responded to this exclusion by creating their own youth culture, which both in its 60s counter-culture form and its later rap/hip-hop form included considerable hostility to and contempt for adults. Adults responded by viewing teens as dangerous: the putative gangs in the 1950s, the counter-culture in the 1960s, the supposed "super predators" of the 1980s, and so on.

In our *cofigurative* culture, many adolescents feel sentenced to years of high school, which offers them a repressive, alienating, and largely meaningless experience. So they look to each other for engagement and meaning. Yet adolescents are not mature human beings, so the culture they create is also adolescent, immature, and often unnecessarily egocentric.

What we need to create, Mead argues, is a *prefigurative* culture, in which the capacity of adolescents to see the world anew—with idealism and creative vision as well as with sometimes unbalanced judgment and critique—and make novel sense of it is valued by adults. In such a culture, teens would be welcomed into adult society as contributors with different strengths and limitations, and teens who were engaged in this way would value the experience and wisdom of adults. Forty years ago Mead saw the destructive divisions and the denial of wisdom that a cofigurative society engenders and argued that we need to move beyond this dead end.

What kinds of experiences and social structures would we offer teens if we understood adolescence rightfully to be a new stage of human development that can allow a more complete unfolding of each human's potential? This is the creative challenge we need to answer today.

Howard Thurman wrote, *"Don't ask what the world needs. Ask what makes you come alive, and go do it. Because what the world needs is people who have come alive."* The evolutionary potential of adolescence as a stage in human development is that for the first time in our species history, we have created societies in which individual human beings can discover what it is that makes them come alive—their gifts, their passions, their callings—and can begin to "go do it." Not later on. Not when they're older. Now, today.

This is exactly what our species needs, to unleash our most profound creativity and capacity, if we intend to evolve through the crises and challenges we have created for ourselves in this century.

Notes

1. Margaret Mead (1970, 1978). *Culture and Commitment: The New Relationships between the Generations in the 1970s.* New York: Columbia University Press.

3 THE COMMON VISION'S GUIDANCE FOR PARENTS

The *common vision* of Rudolf Steiner, Aurobindo Ghose, and Inayat Khan tells us how we can raise and educate our children so that they can embody their potential—so they can access post-modern consciousness in their teens and integral consciousness in their early twenties—and so we can evolve as a species through and beyond the dangers of our current global challenges.

The key lessons of the *common vision* for our time are these:

The common vision's descriptions of human nature and of the course of human becoming in childhood and youth are as valid today as they were in 1910. They provide us with an understanding of who we and our children are as beings—and of who we, and particularly our children, have the potential to become. They also help us to understand the relatively predictable course of our children's and teens' unfoldment through the first twenty-one years of life—and what's possible in terms of the development of their consciousness at the end of this part of the lifespan.

However, we need to recognize that the timing described in the *common vision* of unfoldment is not absolute. Today, at least in North America and Western Europe, the onset of the third era of childhood and youth, the beginning of adolescence, seems to be earlier than what was described by Steiner, Aurobindo, and Inayat Khan. Whether this is the result of spiritual or cultural changes, or some combination of both, is not clear.

Even with this change of timing, the three eras of childhood and youth continue to exist as they are detailed by the *common vision*, as do all of the many interrelationships among the unfoldment of body, emotions, mind, and soul/spirit. We need to gain an understanding of the nature and challenges of each of these eras of unfoldment and then use this understanding to inform the ways in which we nurture and educate children and youth. Each child is unique, yes; **and** each child moves through a relatively predictable course of becoming through the three eras. The more we know of this course, the more effective we can be in supporting the unfoldment of our children.

The most profound element for child raising and education within Steiner's, Aurobindo's, and Inayat Khan's common vision is the understanding that we must have faith in the child's inner teacher, her soul/spirit, to guide her own becoming. Thus, we must provide the child with a safe environment and, within that zone of safety, as much freedom as possible to express and fulfill her own needs.

The inner teacher, the soul/spirit, expresses its intents and needs through the child's will. Here we absolutely need to distinguish between "freedom within safe, developmentally-appropriate boundaries" and "license." Freedom means that, as much as possible, we construct an environment that is safe for the child, given her developmental status and then give her freedom within that safe environment. For example, for the infant who is crawling, we cover the electric outlets and remove breakable items that she might displace and smash. For the seven year old who is playing with friends outdoors, we might set a boundary of staying in our own backyard. For the sixteen year old who is going out for the evening, we might set a curfew time of 12 midnight or 1 AM. Parents must strive to set and maintain safe, developmentally-appropriate boundaries for their child and teen, but within those boundaries we want to give our children freedom. And, of course, the safe boundaries are always changing as the child grows up. Parenting is about letting go in a conscious and measured manner, not too fast and not too slow—and by conscious and careful choice.

Some parents confuse freedom with license. License means freedom to behave as one wishes, especially in a way that results in excessive and harmful behavior. This confusion results when parents perceive the value in giving the child freedom yet they fail to understand the child's simultaneous need for appropriate and safe boundaries. Children who are given license are often distorted by this grant both because their ego development is excessive and they feel inadequately supported and protected by their parents.

The key is freedom within safe and appropriate boundaries— and parents must continually reconsider what those boundaries ought to be. The personal challenge for parents is that we can only enact the teachings of the common vision about freedom with integrity to the extent of our own unfoldment as whole and integrated persons, and no more.

We can only give the child as much respect for her *inner teacher*, as much freedom for her becoming, as the state of our own current unfoldment empowers us. If we extend beyond that limit in our enthusiasm or pride, we will likely betray the understandings of the *common vision* and act out hypocrisy or contradiction, either through indirect or unconscious authoritarian behavior or through the failure to set and maintain needed boundaries.

Thus, we must understand the *common vision* both as an ideal, a goal toward which we strive, and as a practical map toward achieving that goal. As a map, the *common vision* informs us of the steps that lead toward the ideal. Each step that we can enact successfully brings us closer toward the manifestation of the ideal, although we will never achieve it. In taking these steps, we must always stay aware of the intimate connection between our own growth as unfolding persons and our ability to nurture the growth of our children. The more we unfold, the more we will be able to move toward enacting the ideal of the *common vision*.

Only through a parent's or teacher's own spiritual evolution can she or he increase the amount of freedom that she or he can give to the child. Every step the parent or teacher can take toward the ideal, every motion toward greater trust in the *inner teacher* and greater freedom for the child, is worth taking. Every step in this direction is a significant step in the evolutionary process. So the issue is not all or nothing: freedom or its absence. It is as much freedom as possible, with clarity and integrity and enough comfort. This is our most important lesson from the *common vision* as parents.

Just for a moment, draw up an image of a 4-year-old you know or have known who is engaged, determined, focused, creative, confident, and excited. Now imagine what children in the second era of childhood, or youths in the third era, could be like if they could bring this same energy for learning and creating into their lives. If we don't limit or push or mold or direct or confine or terrorize children, there's no reason they can't be as whole, or even more whole, at 10 years or 15 years as many are today at 3 or 4.

The timetables of the *common vision* are not absolutes. They are guidelines and norms. *All children and youth unfold at their own rates, and some do so much more slowly or quickly than most*. In addition, it is very common for a child to unfold at different rates in different aspects of her being.

Each era or stage in the unfoldment of the child and youth must be lived fully. Each must be explored for what it can be and valued for itself, not rushed through quickly or seen only as a step on the way to somewhere else. Each era or stage has its own ultimate value. The principle that guides human growth is not haste or acceleration but the completeness of the unfoldment of the individual's potentials in each era of her life.

As parents and teachers we must understand this principle of becoming and respect its mandate. Sooner is not necessarily better. Each child has her own timetable. What is best for each child is the opportunity to live each era or stage fully, without pressure or compulsion to move on before she is ready to do so.

The common vision explains that children learn most profoundly from who their parents are as people, from the wholeness and rightness of these adults' qualities and actions. To nurture our children more effectively, to help them grow and unfold, we need to work on our own growth as much as that of the next generation. We must strive to become as good examples for them as we can be, for the future is born in the present.

The common vision tells us explicitly that everything that children and youth experience has an impact on who they are and who they become. The system is a seamless whole; nothing experienced by the child is without influence. This understanding informs us that children's experience of media matters tremendously in our hyper-mediated culture. If children watch thousands of hours of violence and advertising on television or spend excessive amounts of time on the web, iPads/tablets, or their smart phones, these images and messages indelibly affect who they are and will become.

Modernist consciousness does not see age-inappropriate or excessive electronic media consumption as the profound threat to children's unfoldment that it is. This is not to condemn electronic media; electronic media are accelerating the evolution of consciousness all over the planet. But for children, electronic media can both limit and misshape unfoldment and become addictive. As parents we cannot transform the mainstream media culture, but we can control, direct, or influence the media experiences our children have, particularly during the first stage of life from birth to age seven. We can be guided both by the precautionary principle—*if a technology has a suspected risk of causing harm to a child, we should err on the side of caution in its use*—and by avoiding the forbidden fruit syndrome—*don't hold the tech toy in front of the child, enjoy it yourself, but forbid your child to use it.* Sometimes this means that parents have to wait until later to use their own tech toys.

For the first two years of life even physicians in the American Academy of Pediatrics recommend the following:

> Pediatricians should urge parents to avoid television viewing for children under the age of 2 years. Although certain television programs may be promoted to this age group, research on early brain development shows that babies and toddlers have a critical need for direct interactions with parents and other significant caregivers

for healthy brain growth and the development of
appropriate social, emotional, and cognitive skills.
Therefore, exposing such young children to television
programs should be discouraged.[1]

The same advice holds true for computer monitors, tablets, smart
phones, and any other forms of electronic imagery.

Once children are two years old, their use of electronic media
should be consciously selected by parents—again, appropriate
boundaries—and limited to relatively short periods of time.
Children in these ages have access to a rich inner life of the
imagination when adults allow and support this unfoldment, and
the articulation and exploration of this inner life is directly tied to
the child's capacity for unfoldment into higher consciousness in
adolescence and young adulthood. It's much more valuable for the
four year old to play out a complex narrative with his imaginary
friend than for the child to play with colors or games on an Ipad.
Over time a deluge of external imagery shuts down the child's
internal imagery, damaging his access to imagination, intuition,
and creativity.

During the second era of childhood, children continue to need
boundaries to be set for them, both in regard to the amount of time
they devote to electronic screens and to the content of electronic
materials, whether this be video games, websites, smart phones,
films, television, or whatever. Of course, the boundaries need to be
adjusted as children grow older. In these years most children
venture forth beyond the family, so parents need to understand
that their capacity for control of their child's media diet is
inevitably diminished. Most children spend time in the homes of
their friends, and their friends' parents may have different values
when it comes to media. Parents can still talk with their child about
what he may have seen at a friend's home and engage that child in
reflection on and critique of its messages, but parents need to seek
a balance between protecting the child and trusting his judgment.

***We must always recognize our children as beings who have the
potential to—indeed, who are likely to, if we are successful as parents—evolve beyond us.*** Given this understanding of evolution and

unfoldment, we must truly be open to learning from our children, from the very moment of their birth and in every subsequent moment, as well as helping them to learn and unfold. This is what Margaret Mead understood when she described our evolutionary need to create a *prefigurative culture*, in which children learn from their parents, other adults, and each other, and adults learn from their children and other members of their children's generation.

Lessons for the First Era

Here are the lessons in particular for parents of children who are in the first era of life, from birth through ages 6-7 years.

The *common vision* tells us that the child in the first era belongs not in school but in the family. And yet we live in a culture in which most of our young children spend considerable amounts of their lives in daycare and preschool environments. How do we reconcile this teaching with our social reality?

There is nothing ultimately natural or necessarily desirable about the isolated nuclear family, or even about the multigenerational family. For most of human history, children grew up in tribal or clan groups, interacting intensively with other children and adults within the group. So the central element offered by the *common vision* in its essence is not the nuclear family as such, or even the multigenerational family. Rather, it is the description of the child's need in the first era of life to be in a family-like context, a social setting of love, safety, stability, consistency, and a high quality of care. Within this context, she needs to have as much freedom and opportunity for self-direction available to her as possible, with little competition or pressure to achieve. This teaching of the *common vision* gives us a detailed model for the kind of day-care and pre-school settings we need to create for our children, with love and stability of relationships over time as the most important elements.

The *common vision* tells us that every child and youth learns from her interactions with the adults in her life. We need to understand clearly that the child in the first era of life, the first seven years or

39

so, learns most profoundly from an often explicit imitation of those around her. If a child spends most of her conscious time in day care or pre-school, she will learn profoundly from her caregiver(s) or teacher(s) in that environment. There is nothing inherently wrong with this, but it is a reality that so-called *quality time* cannot change. *Quality is important in the relationship between adult and child, but quantity is undoubtedly more powerful with a child who learns through imitation.*

The *common vision* requires this of us as parents: if we put our child in day-care, we must place her with an adult who will provide her with as good a basis for imitation as we can find and who will stay in relationship with the child over several years. This is a minimum requirement. The step beyond this requires social change so that both mothers and fathers can spend much more time with their young children without sacrificing their prospects of obtaining satisfying work. This change demands a more flexible workplace in which the needs of children and parents are more highly valued. It also calls for a society less concerned with wealth and material goods and more able to find meaning and satisfaction in human relationships and expression.

The *common vision* tells us that if we want our children to have an intimate relationship with nature in their teen and adult years, we need to anchor them in a deep relationship with nature during the first era. Particularly from ages 3-7 years, children are open to profound and intimate connection with nature: with plants and animals, yes, but also with the earth and the sky and clouds and the horizon. Post-modern consciousness reminds us that humans are nature just as much as the trees and the ocean. If we want our children to come of age both with that understanding and with a deep emotional tie to the natural world, we need to give them many opportunities to experience nature directly in the first era.

Lessons for the Second and Third Eras

The fundamental guidance for parents remains the same in both of these eras of childhood and youth: give your child as much freedom as possible within safe and appropriate boundaries. Of course, the first challenge comes in gaining clarity about what those boundaries should be. The second challenge is maintaining the awareness that your child is growing and evolving at an unpredictable rate, with periods of relative stability alternating with periods of dramatic growth and, at times, temporary regression, so the safe and appropriate boundaries need recalibration and alteration regularly—but on an irregular schedule.

During the second era the child usually becomes more independent and expands his social life to include more time in the homes of his friends, including meals and sleepovers. Here parents need to find a middle way, continuing to assert their core values in relation to important elements in their child's experience, for example, nutrition, sleep, responsibilities, and exposure to mass media culture, but also acknowledging that their child will—and must—enter the larger social world which will increasingly be beyond his parents' control. Too much control may easily become counter-productive, generating resistance in the child. Boundaries that are too lax may promote license.

In the second (ages 6-7 through puberty) and third (puberty through age 21 years) eras of life, education takes on a larger role in children's and teens' lives. The *common vision* tells us that much of what goes on in our schools today is antithetical to the growth and unfoldment of the child and youth. School as we all know it was a social invention of modernist consciousness, initially at the end of the 18th century in Prussia and in the 1840s in the US. Schools incorporated many progressive, child-friendly elements when they were first invented. For example, children in school were not working 14-hour days in factories, and in the 20th century schools gave many children and teens access to social mobility and enhanced consciousness. At the same time, schools also always included what we now judge as harmful elements of social control, for example, the way in which the schedule dominates all activities and the authoritarian governance of almost all public schools.

Despite all the changes in our culture and consciousness since the 1920s when the final version of the industrial school paradigm gained its climax form, conventional schools, both public and private, remain committed to an industrial process in which knowledge is viewed as a standardized commodity. These schools now work primarily for the purposes of limiting consciousness to the current norms. This antiquated character of schools has led to a growing tension between the lives of young people outside school and what they are required to experience within, intensifying the felt sense in our society that our schools are not "working."

Since the early 1990s American political and corporate leaders have accurately perceived the slow disintegration of the industrial school paradigm. Rather than exploring how to create post-modern schools, they have worked to intensify the repressive, destructive elements of the modernist school through the following:

- Standardization of the school curriculum, first in each state and then throughout the nation through the so-called Common Core, thus repressing creativity and personalization of learning;
- The abusive implementation of standardized tests, with the same results as the above but also penalizing students and teachers who resist standardization;
- The implementation of so-called merit pay in which teachers are paid to raise students' test scores and, raising the stakes even more, tying teachers' pay and job security directly to the test scores of their students.

Each of these features is designed to intensify centralized control over what students and teachers do in school. And in the implementing these various industrial school measures, both political parties are equally responsible and equally hostile to the evolution of human consciousness.

There are some schools, however, that are aligned with the needs and potentials of the child and youth as revealed by the *common vision*, although sadly not very many are public schools.

- Self-identified "***democratic schools***" usually embrace the common vision's core value of freedom within appropriate boundaries, as do self-identified "open schools." Many of these schools identify with the Sudbury Valley School in

Framingham, Massachusetts, which itself was inspired by Summerhill, A. S. Neill's "freedom school" in England.

- *Waldorf schools* were founded by Rudolf Steiner in 1919 and have grown into an international network of schools. Waldorf schools offer a brilliantly post-modern and, in some ways, integral curriculum and usually have a dedicated, motivated, and well-prepared faculty. However, one concern with Waldorf schools is that the movement remains tied to the curriculum that Steiner created in 1919 for German children and has no formal mechanism for evolving its curriculum and principles. Steiner himself believed in the universal nature of evolution as the central energy in life on Earth, and it is likely that were he alive today, he would suggest a significantly different school curriculum and structure than is featured in current Waldorf schools.

- *Montessori schools*: Maria Montessori accessed much, though not all, of the *common vision*, so schools that embody her school model faithfully do embrace post-modern values of appropriate freedom, personalization, and community. However, the "Montessori" brand is not trademarked and anyone who has Montessori training can open a "Montessori school." Parents need to carefully evaluate each specific Montessori school to see if it actually does implement Maria Montessori's model faithfully. Also Montessori's model, while brilliant, is also dated in an evolutionary sense, since it has not evolved since 1915.

- *Reggio Emilia* is another post-modern school model, started by Loris Malaguzzi and the parents of children who lived in and near the city of Reggio Emilia in Italy after World War II. The destruction from the war, parents believed, necessitated a new approach to teaching their children. They felt that it is in the early years of development that children are forming who they are as an individual. This led to creation of a program based on the principles of respect, responsibility, and community. In Reggio schools children are invited to explore and discover in a supportive and enriching environment. Thus, much of the curriculum is derived from the interests of the children. The key principles, profoundly post-modern in character, are these:

- Children must have some meaningful control over the direction of their learning.
- Children must be able to learn through experiences of touching, moving, listening, seeing, and hearing.
- Children have engaging relationships with other children and with material items in the world that children can explore.
- Children must have endless ways and opportunities to express themselves, particularly through aesthetic vehicles.

- **EdVisions** is a network of high schools in twelve states in the U.S.A., most of which are charter schools. EdVisions schools focus on enhancing relationships and building relevant learning environments that empower students, parents and teachers to make choices. These learning environments utilize self-directed, project-based learning to build student autonomy through relevant learning opportunities; create student belongingness through full-time advisories; and empower teachers via teacher-led and democratically governed schools. Unfortunately the Edvisions schools are all subject to the control of the standards-and-testing regimes that states have imposed and to the demands of the Common Core and its testing requirements. These forces inevitably push these schools away from their espoused values.

- **Enki Education** is a new post-modern form, created by Beth Sutton and her colleagues. Enki offers a unique and innovative classroom and homeschool Global Cultures curriculum in which all academic learning is introduced through the arts. Enki is based on a Developmental Immersion-Mastery model. The child is immersed in all subject areas through storytelling, arts, and activities. From this rich base, the child's skills and understanding develop to mastery. Both the homeschool and the classroom curricula are carefully chosen to be in harmony with the child's development.

- **SelfDesign,** founded by Brent Cameron and colleagues, is a supported home education program that inspires and nurtures "enthusiasm-based, holistic learning of and by children." The program assists and supports parents as they encourage their children to design and enact their own learning agenda, based on curiosity and enthusiasm. SelfDesign incorporates elements from both postmodern and integral consciousness. The SelfDesign Learning Community was founded in British Columbia in Canada in 2002 and now engages more than 2500 families in a unique expression of public education.

School is a modernist social form. Everywhere on the planet, as societies achieve modernist economic and social structures, they send their children to modernist, industrial schools.

While it is unlikely that "school" will disappear any time soon, as the number of parents who center on post-modern consciousness reaches a critical mass in the most "developed" societies, these parents will gain the will and the political power to transform "school" into a new social form that better fits postmodern values. We probably will not call this new social form "school."

Until we reach that critical mass, parents with post-modern consciousness will have to find education for their children outside the normative public school systems.

The Common Vision and the Role of Culture

The *common vision* speaks about the nature and potential of all children, all human beings. Yet culture also plays a significant role in the growth and learning of children and youths. Culture gives each child a set of understandings for making sense of his or her world and powerfully affects each child's perception, meaning-making, and behavior. In the United States, despite the historic image of the "melting pot" as the forge for a single mainstream culture, many racial, ethnic, social class, and regional groups continue to embody and enact their own distinct versions of American culture—for example, African-American, Chinese-American, and Appalachian cultures—which exist along with mainstream culture. In addition, both mainstream culture and the various ethnic, racial, social class, and regional cultures define and create roles for young people based on gender.

As parents we must become as conscious as we can of our own cultural values and norms. We must honor and offer to our children the elements in our own home cultures that enrich life and unfoldment. At the same time we must identify cultural elements that inhibit or deny our children's exercise of appropriate freedom and self-direction, and if we truly seek the unfoldment of our children's potential, we must abandon these inhibitory cultural elements as much as we can.

A Word of Caution

The *common vision* is not perfect or finished or complete. We can always learn more. Evolution continues. We must draw on our knowledge of the *common vision* but always in relation to our own insight, discrimination, and common sense. We must not make it "an answer" but keep it as a guide in relationship with our own unfolding selves.

The Common Vision: A Path to Co-evolution

The *common vision* of Rudolf Steiner, Aurobindo Ghose, and Inayat Khan is a set of directions for co-evolution, for our conscious participation in the process of ongoing evolution on this planet. It is also a set of directions for human survival if we choose to recognize and act upon it. We must grow and evolve, or we will surely perish. The *common vision* gives us a path to follow that will nurture this growth for ourselves and our children, a path that leads both to survival and to co-evolution.

Notes

1. *Pediatrics.* November 2011, Volume 128, Issue 5.

4 JANET AND BARRY LIA

The next seven chapters introduce you to parents whose engagement with their child(ren) has been guided by a consciousness that is inclusive of all or much of the *common vision*. From these parents you'll hear about the ways in which these insights about human nature and human becoming were translated into the daily lives of parenting and family.

You will also gain an introduction to six late teens/young adults who have experienced this quality of parenting as they have grown through childhood and adolescence.

Please note that the children discussed in these interviews grew up just a few short years ago before the current explosion of smart phones, texting, iPads, Facebook, and Twitter. The technologies you'll hear discussed in these interviews are television, movies, computers, computer games, and the Internet. Even as new communication technologies take up more space at the center of our lives and increase our virtual reach, both near and far, the principles of the common vision remain the same for childhood and adolescence.

Janet and Barry Lia

Janet and Barry live in Seattle. They have two daughters, Anna and Emmy.

Janet: One of the most important things for me was protecting early childhood, from infancy on. Protecting the kids from too many sense impressions, especially media sense impressions. And I wanted to give a very strong sense of rhythm to each young child, a sense of rhythm to each day. I wanted to bring a real consciousness to the care I gave them. So we were pretty conservative with that with both kids until eight months or so. We didn't take them out to the mall or even to the grocery store. Even after eight months it was quite limited for awhile longer. And then as far as protecting from the media and all these influences, we're still doing that today, and Anna, our oldest, is 13 now.

Barry: But we haven't been purists, by any means.

Janet: No. They've seen TV, they've been to the movies. But they never went to the movies until they were five. And even today, Emmy's eight, and she's only been to probably half a dozen movies in her life.

Barry: She'll see videos at home.

Janet: But we try to screen the videos first to see if they're okay for her.

Barry: There's a stage with young children—a stage of imitation, emulation, mimicry. And you don't want media to be the model for that imitation. If they're just imitating garbage, they'll grow up with garbage.

Janet: And the media gets in the way of imaginative play, which should come from inside the child, not from the media images.

Barry describes the most fundamental quality of children in the first era; they perceive whatever takes place before them and they imitate it. Janet identifies one key problem that media create when experienced by young children; media images fill the child's mind, displacing images that come from the child's own being.

Janet: Anna will be in eighth grade at the Waldorf school. She has an interest in the larger culture, yes. But we don't have music playing all the time, and we don't have TV on in the background. We gave her a CD player a couple years ago, and she has 20 or 30 CD's, but she really doesn't play them that much. She likes to go to the mall, but she's not interested in just wandering around endlessly. She's interested in popular culture. She looks at the teen magazines, but I don't think she's obsessed with it, and she's not taken in by it. I think a lot of that has to do with our influence. We don't buy into all that stuff. But you can't negate the fact that children are their own individuals, too, and so she has her own good sense.

Barry: There's certainly some tension in this, too. She doesn't always do what we'd prefer.

Both Janet and Barry recognize the tension between giving Anna the freedom to become her self and their desire to provide protective boundaries. There is no resolution for this tension, just an ongoing dialogue between these two equally important values.

Janet: And, of course, we do set limits for her. There have been times when she's wanted to watch TV and we've said, "Look, you know it's a school day. You know what the rule is in the house." And even when she was a little girl, I can remember her wanting to get a Barbie, and I wasn't hot on that idea. And I think I said, "It's not our style." In the end she did have some kind of doll that was similar to a Barbie. And she passed through it, and it was okay. I didn't want to be too dogmatic and say, "Absolutely no Barbies."

Barry: We were trying not to create forbidden fruits. We wanted her to learn to see through these kind of things—Barbie—not just to see it the way we do, but to make her own way through things, so she can see for herself how things are.

As Barry notes, sometimes the identification of a "forbidden fruit" in a child's mind can be more harmful than allowing the child to have an experience or possession that the parent finds undesirable. Often, as Janet explains, once the child does gain access to the desired object, she finds that it has less value and/or satisfaction than she thought it would.

Barry: But it's not like there is no rebellion. She's pushing against organic foods.

Janet: Yeah, she does rebel against that. "Why do we have to eat organic all the time?" she asks.

Barry: So we indulge her rebellion sometimes, and then sometimes we don't.

Janet: Emmy is eight. And she's still so young that she's just going along with whatever is presented to her. It's easy. Knock on wood. Our kids have totally different personalities. Anna's very serious and more of a thinker, pensive. And Emmy's still very light-hearted and sanguine. Anna does not want to go to the Waldorf high school; she's told us that. She wants, what did she say, a real world experience. And that's another place where we're not going to try to force the issue. Neither of us see any reason to try and force that because it would just be setting ourselves for a terrible teenage time.

This is an example of parents opening the boundaries as the adolescent asserts her own desires.

Janet: Barry's father was worried about Anna because she wasn't reading (in first grade).

Barry: Oh, yeah, he sent "Hooked on Phonics." That was an issue because her reading was so late in his view.

Janet: She didn't start reading until third grade, and that was a big deal for Barry's dad.

It's not unusual for grandparents or other family members to assert developmental expectations for a child that ignore the unique trajectory of each human being's unfoldment. Modernist consciousness asserts that all children should be able to read by the end of the first grade, but there's no scientific support for this assertion. In contrast, much evidence from the lives of children who were allowed to learn to read when they chose to do so clearly demonstrates that what matters most is motivation, not chronological age. Given access to natural learning, many children progress from beginning reading to high levels of reading competence in only a few years.

Barry: So he sent that. We cracked it open, and the stuff's terribly boring. We never used it. One answer to his concern is her writing. You should see her write. She writes better than she reads.

Janet: But she reads just fine. She's not a person who likes to read, but she's perfectly able to read.

Barry: Emmy is teaching herself to read right now.

Janet: Yeah, she's learning to read now. She's going into second grade now. So it won't be an issue with her. She's older for her class. She's already eight, going into second grade, whereas Anna was seven in second grade.

Barry: But she also has her older sister as an example, so she's been doing a lot on her own initiative just to pick things up.

Janet: I have always felt that the ideal is to offer the child a lot of aesthetic choices and quality choices for play. So we've had very simple toys here—blocks, wooden things, pieces of cloth—and our kids have been immensely happy with that. But also we have had plastic, like these Legos, which I have found to be wonderful toys. This is not the only thing I'd want them to play with, but they stay shiny, they don't break, and they're always put together in new and interesting ways. So I've never had any problem with those. We like the bigger ones because they're more of a tactile experience than those little, tiny things. But I think that you can't run away from plastic. I wouldn't go out and buy some of these ugly figurines, whatever they're called. I couldn't afford to get silk scarves for the kids to play with. So we went to the thrift store and got whatever was colorful. I'm sure we had plenty of polyester in those scarves.

Barry: We wouldn't have Legos as the only toy. It teaches some things. It teaches a mechanical thinking, in a sense. They fit this way, and they only orient in certain ways. I wouldn't want that to be the only thing they could learn, but it is something to learn and to know about as well. We've never written down and thought out clear guidelines for all of this about toys. It's more feeling and intuition.

Janet: There was a time when Anna was really into these things called My Little Ponies. And I never thought those were so great. They were this plastic, rubbery thing with long hair. And yet I completely let her have My Little Ponies, and she had her collection of Little Ponies and she thoroughly enjoyed them. She played very imaginatively with them.

Barry: And she had sticker books. There's this categorization that they do with these books. They have the categories. Here's the fuzzies, these pages are the such-and-such, the vegetables. And that's useful.

Janet: Now, Emmy is into Beanie Babies. And the thing I object to about Beanie Babies is that it's just a matter of collecting them. That's what bugs me, it's a marketing thing. But I don't say you can't get that Beanie Baby. They do play with them a little though. It's important to her for some reason. And it's not worth making a huge issue out of it, or denying her that for your own judgment, unless you thought it would harm her. For example, I would deny my children video games. We don't have video games, and we don't allow them to play on the computer. I deny them that. And to this day, I don't like them to sit and while away the time on the computer. But why do I deny that? That's because I really believe that that is taking away from something positive in their lives. They could be off playing or writing or reading, or being with their friends.

Janet asserts several boundaries that are fundamental to her values as to what kinds of experiences are the most beneficial for her children.

Barry: Emmy has made a handful of paint software pictures on the computer.

Janet: She's experienced that, but we wouldn't let her do it all the time. So I would deny that. I would also deny certain kinds of music, if I felt it was needed. I think some of it is actively harmful.

Barry: The larger society thinks that because it's on the market, it must be it's okay. But a lot of it is not okay. I want to offer protection and guidance to my kids, the best I can.

Janet: We're supposed to be the ones who know better. We're supposed to guide them.

Barry: But we are also trying to listen and allow our children free expression.

Barry and Janet often express the two sides of this central polarity: freedom within safe boundaries. When one parent conveys one side, the other parent provides the opposite side.

Janet: For example, today we went shoe shopping, and Anna wanted to get these shoes which I just think are worthless, and sort of hideous, too. And she pointed out to me—she kept asking me—how do you like these shoes? And I kept saying, "No, no, not those. How do you like these?" And she would say, "Oh, Mom, forget that." So she pointed out to me that every pair of shoes that she liked, I didn't. And I said, "Well, that's true, so you're just going to have to pick out the ones that you feel you'll like and that you'll be happy with." And she did, and I don't like them and I'm not happy with them, but I did get them for her because she is her own person. She has her own taste. And it's not that important, because that's just a physical appearance. I hope she doesn't want to pierce her ears in six places, but she probably will, and we'll have to just say, "Well, do it safely." I want to preserve our relationship, and I kind of relish her independent nature.

Barry: I want to honor the relationship, honor and respect. For instance, helping around the house. We just sort of kept putting the idea out to Anna and saying, "This would be useful for us." But we haven't dictated it.

Janet: Although she has certain chores.

Barry: Anna has some chores, yes. But now she's starting to pick up and do things, and be proud of it. And I'm proud of her for doing it, and I try to foster that.

Janet: Just recently she and I have been talking about sex. Just the other day she asked me when I lost my virginity. I'll tell you, it was hard for me at first to talk about it, and I actually wanted to stretch the time forward. And I started to talk with her about being able to please herself, and I was remembering what it was like for me when I was 13, and all the things that come up. And I really relish the fact that she'll even listen to me, or that she's even interested in my sex life. And you have to go really gingerly, because you can easily cross a boundary that is really too much for them. I don't want to propel her forward in this, but I do want to face things before it becomes an issue.

This kind of intimacy between teenager and parent is not what we see as the norm in our society. Yet here is a teen who seeks out her mother for this conversation, because she knows both that her mother respects her as her own person and that her mother will tell her the truth.

Barry: So much of what teenagers face, so much of what they do— it's decided by their maturity at that moment. And you hope they'll have the background, the basis, the grounding, to weather these things, to make good decisions.

Janet: Some kids at 18 have had such a poor preparation, they can make terrible choices, whereas another kid at 15, who's quite strong and confident—they can know what's the right thing to do for themselves. Modern culture exposes children to TV and the Internet completely uncensored, from a very young age. Two-year olds working the remote and seeing all this stuff. And never does it occur to these parents that this might be something that's damaging and addictive, that the kids will never have the ability to discern the fact that there is something wrong here, because that's what they've had their whole life.

****

This next interview was conducted a year later.

Janet: Emmy is reading now. And Anna is fully into teenage-hood. She is quite challenging. She's moody. She's very independent. She is disrespectful. She's also responsible and intelligent and dependable. She really expresses desires and wants them fulfilled right now.

Janet describes the first third of the third era: "In the first third of this era, the youth experiences an intense inconsistency over which she has little control." Even an early adolescent such as Anna, who has had the benefit of conscious parenting from both parents in her childhood, is subject to the de-centering humans experience in this profound passage out of childhood. In this stage progresses toward adulthood at time; at other times she regresses into previous emotional levels, including those from many years prior to her current chronological age. The maturity level of her behavior is inconsistent and unpredictable, and the behavior is sometimes beyond her conscious control.

Janet: Anna wants to go to the public high school next year, and that's fine. She wants to experience the kind of direction you get from teachers in public school. She wants the experience of culture, on the broader scale, to be mixed with kids from many different cultural backgrounds. And she wants facilities. She does not want to go to a school that has no dark room and no gym and no band.

Barry: Anna is not one of those achiever academic types. She does her work well, and she does beautiful work. She takes a long time doing things.

Janet: We see her as really well balanced. She can do math, she can read, she can write. She does her work, but there's a lot of other things going on for her beyond that.

Barry: A couple of times at the table Anna has said, "Oh, I don't believe in God." And I think it's this notion of some standard image of God.

Janet: We're not church goers.

Barry: We haven't said anything one way or another. So then she carries her thoughts further.

Janet: You can hear in what she's saying that she believes in something higher. She recognizes something higher. But the notion of it being some kind of patriarchal hierarchy is absurd to her. Yet she alludes to believing in some omnipotent greater good.

One clear sign of a teenager beginning to access post-modern consciousness is this sort of description of "God" or "the divine"— "something higher."

Janet: So it's really interesting, because it seems like she's saying this stuff at first to see how we will react. I've had some conversations with her about sex and drugs. I've talked to her a bit about this and said my concerns about what it's like for a young woman, and I try to explain the things that I went through, which she does not want to hear. "Don't even go there, Mom." But at the same time she's trying to consult with me. I think she does have better sense, but it's not fully formed yet.

Here again is Anna's ambivalence. Sometimes she wants to push her mother away; at other times she wants to engage her in trusting, intimate conversation. At this point in their unfoldment, many teens who have not had the benefit of such conscious parenting lose their connection with their parents and focus all of their identity-development work both in pushing away from their parents and in gaining acceptance in their peer group. Yet this disconnection is neither inevitable nor desirable. Most of the time Janet and Barry can tolerate Anna's ambivalence and inconsistency, and this tolerance allows Anna to go back and forth but stay connected to her parents.

Barry: When I'm listening to Anna and she goes off with some idea, I'm holding back on offering my own knowledge in order to listen to her, to make a space for listening. I hope she'll say something that I feel positive about—but even when she doesn't, I still want to hold that space for listening and not just jump in with my belief. I think that it's important to hold your values and to express them eventually, but just not to immediately kill the issue by squashing things with your values.

Barry offers valuable guidance for parents of teens: listen first, talk later.

Barry: For example, the food. Anna is always wanting junk food now. I try not to push too much against that. I gripe and grumble about it, yes. So I kind of work that way with it, that it's going to be this encounter of push and shove and step back and listen. And it's going to go on for awhile. But I think it works.

Janet: One of the things that Anna and I can share now is shopping. And that is just torture for me, I hate going shopping. It's not something that when I was a teenager I enjoyed either. So I find it really taxing, but at the same time I can kind of enjoy Anna when we're shopping. One day over vacation she wanted to make me up. So I did it, and I felt like she was five again and she was making me up. I said I would never wear what she put all over me, but it was really nice. And I look at this make-up thing, which I was never attracted to in my life. But this make-up with Anna was different. It's so funny, the things you have to get into for your kids.

Janet: I think that everything that a parent does when kids are really young, before the age of seven—this is what you're building on now when they're in their teens. What didn't happen then, you can't go back and put in now. This is not to say it's hopeless, but if you've done that early preparation, that early work, then it's so much easier. What's in there in the child comes out so she can build on it.

Janet articulates another key element of the common vision: that nurturance given to the child in the first era—freedom within safe boundaries, the opportunity to live out her first era qualities, particularly exploration and the imagination—provides a foundation of being for the child as she grows through the second and third eras.

Janet: I clearly can see how Anna is really unfolding. And I can see it in terms of her thinking abilities, and the different imaginative stages she's gone through, and now getting into the spiritual life. And I also see it in terms of her personality becoming more formed and more fully expressed, although it certainly isn't complete yet. In early childhood, she lived very much in her fantasy world, so she was always creating another world. She was completely absorbed in her imaginative life. And then with school, the early school years you could start to see her intellectual abilities starting to develop, and she was finding out how she as herself could differentiate from her friends. And eventually, slowly, getting up to the point, maybe in fifth or sixth grade, where she could say, "No, I don't like that, I'm not going to do that, don't talk to me that way." She could stand up for herself. And that's when the personality began to manifest much more distinctly. And now she's beginning to think about spiritual concepts and what she believes. Anna is extremely challenging for adults but in a mostly positive way. She is independent thinking, and she is testing the adults to be true to their words.

One of the key tasks of unfoldment for teens is to explore and test the veracity and integrity of the adults in their world. This can be painful for the adults at times, but it is essential if the teen is to develop her own capacity for truth-making.

****

This next interview was conducted two years later.

Barry: Anna is sixteen now. She was at Nathan Hale High School for two years, and now she's going to Seattle Central Community College for her Running Start program. She's very challenged there. She's a lot more enthusiastic about learning. [Running Start is a program in Washington State that allows high school juniors and seniors to take courses in a local junior college. Course credits earned in Running Start count both toward high school graduation and as college credits.]

Janet: She's working hard, and she's doing really, really well. Just yesterday, she got her portfolio back in English, and the teacher wrote on it, "Wow, I hope you go to a four-year university that deserves you!" And the teacher wants to use Anna's essays and her journal entries in the packet that she gives to other students. So we were really proud of her.

Barry: After the Waldorf school, she liked Hale at first. She really liked the diversity of kids. She met African-American kids and Japanese-American kids. She was very involved with other kinds of people that she hadn't known much before. But then after a year or so, she was ready to get out of Hale.

Janet: There was very little individual recognition. And sometimes teachers questioned her work. She would do a really beautiful drawing in English in addition to some writing assignment, and then the teacher would say, "Did you really do that?" She was embarrassed. "You can ask my mom if you want, you know," she'd reply. They didn't value the beauty that she was putting into the work. It was like they said, "That's nice, but don't spend time on that." The Hale teachers' standards were very much lower than what she was used to. What they considered good enough was shocking to her, compared to what she had been used to in the Waldorf school.

Barry: And they didn't value the aesthetics of what she did.

Janet: By the end of Waldorf school she really wanted a larger social group than just one class. But in reality, even in a larger high school, kids keep to a pretty small social group. And she didn't find that many kids who she wanted to know. So at the community college, it's really different. She goes to her classes, and she leaves. It's not for a social connection. And most of the students are so much older, in their late twenties and more. She has a job now, too. She's working at the Body Shop.

Barry: She's also involved in a program called Teen Read. It involves tutoring elementary school kids. It's a great program. She had done that for two school years and a summer and also worked as a teacher's aide in summer school.

Janet: I think we're through the most challenging part with Anna. Once she got close to 16, things started to really improve.

Janet describes the movement from the first third of the adolescent era, the tumultuous period, into the middle third, a calmer and more stable time for teens who have a solid foundation on which to build a new identity. With appropriate nurture and support during the first third, the teen can be very successful in beginning to discover who she is as a more independent person during the middle third of adolescence.

Janet: We have learned though through this last couple of years that you have to be very clear about your expectations as far as going out. You can't leave a lot of assumptions open that it will work out. We had to learn to insist that if you're going out with so-and-so and you're going to be back at such-and-such a time, then if anything changes, we need to know. So we had to learn all these extra little threads to pull through.

In these teenage years, appropriate boundaries still matter greatly.

Janet: We've also had to learn to relax our fears some about what might happen to her out there and give her a certain amount of freedom to take risks and do things that we wouldn't like so much, with the trust that she'll have her experiences and find her way to what's correct. We've trusted her—

Parents also need to continue to let go.

Barry: And she does appreciate being trusted. She's said that.

Janet: One thing that she has helped us with is that she said, "Mom, I've never lied to you. I've told you what I want to do, and I am telling you the truth."

Another signal of accessing post-modern consciousness in adolescents is this fierce allegiance to the truth.

Janet: There were things that she wanted to do that I didn't like, like go to a club. That didn't fit in with my picture and my desire for her, and I didn't like it. I was worried about it. But we let her go, and she did it two or three times and that was enough of that. So I'm grateful that it didn't become a whole subculture of her life.

Barry: It was something that she became disenchanted with on her own. Thank goodness.

The Lias continue in their efforts not to create a forbidden fruit in Anna's mind. Clubbing for the 15 year old is like Barbie for the five year old.

Janet: There have been other issues, for example, curfew. We have relaxed what we thought was reasonable. When I was a kid, I thought 12 o'clock midnight at night was good enough. But that wasn't good enough for Anna. She would want to be out till 1:00 AM or sometimes 2:00. And at first I was just so against that, but then I realized that it would be better that she would tell me this and that we could figure out safe ways for this to take place than to get into this power struggle, which would ultimately end up with us losing. Sometimes she says maybe we want to be out till 1:00, and then she calls up when she gets to her friend's house and it's 11:30 and she says, "There was nothing to do, so we're in." I don't know, maybe we've been lucky.

Barry: Now she can drive, which adds a new feature.

Janet: But she's more reasonable, too. She doesn't feel the need or maybe the desire to go out like she wanted to when she was 15, to break out. Maybe she has the freedom now, and just having that is enough to satisfy something. She's more responsible, too, and takes her own initiative and gets these things done. I don't mix in much, unless she asks for it. Also what we really enjoy now is that we can have adult discussions with her. We had a great discussion one night about spirituality and religion. A deep discussion. One really vital thing that I have learned as a parent is that when your teen gets interested in things that you're not interested in, get involved with them.

Janet's voice of wisdom—how to stay connected to your adolescent child.

Janet: For example, I spent a lot of time during the past two years or so shopping with Anna. At times it was gruesome for me, but I knew that this was an interest she had, and although I don't want to foster some kind of value that I'm not connected to, I want to remain connected with her. So if your son gets into fly fishing and it's not your thing, if you want to remain connected through this period, then you take an interest in it and actively develop that in yourself. And it got a lot better with me when I finally could say to myself not "Oh, no, another weekend at the mall," but "I'm going to go and help her pick out things and find things." I could tolerate the music in the stores, and I didn't have a headache when I came home.

Barry: I usually sat on the bench in the walkway.

****

Barry: Emmy is 11 now. She's in the Waldorf school in fifth grade.

Janet: She's just starting to bud into her pubescence, and it shows. She doesn't want to go to school so much anymore. The usual. I recognize these signs this time.

Barry: There's a lot of challenges. She says, "I'm learning to read music, read books, read Spanish, read Japanese. Everybody wants me to read."

Janet: She also says, "I don't want to lose my imagination. I used to be able to take a leaf and create a whole world in my imagination." So she recognizes what's happening.

Barry: And that reading affected it, learning to read.

Janet: Emmy definitely has more exposure to mainstream, modern pop culture and music than Anna did at that age, because she sees and hears it with Anna.

An obvious yet challenging fact: every child beyond the first born has his or her experience affected by the older child(ren) in the family. So each child's path of unfoldment is indeed unique. Same parents, but a different family.

Barry: So she's singing those pop songs all the time now.

Janet: And we don't try to protect her from too much of that because she loves her sister very much; they have a really close relationship. And they can share this listening to music, and they both enjoy it and that's a good thing for them. So we still don't want her to watch MTV, or much of any TV.

Barry: Exposure to that is much more of a concern.

Janet: But she inevitably has more exposure to popular culture than Anna had.

Barry: Anna still shares some and benefits from Emmy's being a child, her fantasy life.

Janet: And Anna protects Emmy, too, She'll say, "Oh, you don't need to buy into that crap, Emmy. Or don't let them try to get you to do whatever."

Barry: Anna can be a mentor.

Janet: Yes, Anna is really good at that. She says to Emmy, "You don't need to wear makeup; let those other girls do it. That's just stupid for girls your age to do that." Emmy right now is a total homebody. She does not like shopping, yet. She gets all her clothes from her sister. And she's not one who wants to go to the mall with friends. She has this moral struggle with herself about watching TV. She's drawn to it, but she knows that she doesn't want to do it. And she'll say, "I wish I hadn't watched TV. Tomorrow, please don't let me go downstairs and watch TV."

Barry: She understands our condemnation of TV, our speaking unfavorably of it, and maybe she recognizes her own lethargy when she watches. But we do have the TV and we leave it up to her at this point.

Janet: She doesn't feel that good after she watches.

Barry: Emmy started reading in third grade. She mostly picked it up on her own. It's not been fast.

Janet: This year her teacher said, "Now's the time for Emmy to practice reading." And she does practice reading, but it isn't a real strong interest. She'd much rather still be active and play in her imagination.

Barry: She's not one of those to just curl up with a book. She does see others who read much better, and it's a bit of a concern to her. And I just tell her it's a matter of practice, don't worry.

Janet: It never bothered Anna so much, or she never voiced it. But they were both very, quote, slow to develop really strong academic capacities.

Barry: Yes, and now Anna is doing excellent college level work when she's sixteen.

There is no correlation between how quickly a child learns to read initially and her intellectual capacities in adolescence. As with every other quality of the unfolding child, what's desirable is fullness of unfoldment, not speed.

Janet: Anna usually wants to show her papers to us. It's like a vicarious pleasure when your child is writing her thoughts and you get to read them. One paper that she wrote that the professor wanted to use was on the World Trade Organization. It was such a well-analyzed position. And she wrote another essay comparing organic agriculture to conventional agriculture, and all the proponents of both sides. Naturally, I think you could see that she was more in favor of sustainable agriculture.

Janet: My greatest hope for my children is that they grow up to be happy, well adjusted individuals and that they have relationships with other people that are happy and that they have family that they can grow and be together with. That is my biggest hope for them, that their world of relationships be healthy and productive. And whether they become fashion designers or car mechanics or world leaders is really secondary to me. I want them to live in the world in a way that's in keeping with love.

Barry: I think happiness derives largely from serving and giving to others. So whatever they do, I imagine that would be part of it.

Janet: But so many people have difficulty when they grow up. We know how difficult it is to find a partner and to make your marriage work, and then your family relationships can become so dysfunctional, your work relationships—I always say, how can we have world peace if we can't get along in our own living room? And so that just seems to me so fundamental. You do want your children to be capable of achieving what they want out of life. And you're very pleased when your kid is labeled the smart one. That feels great for a moment. But if they should get a job that made a lot of money, what are they going to do with the money? So the main thing is what kind of people are they learning to be? I've said a few prayers over these past few years about my teenage children: "Please, God, don't let her get pregnant or some communicable, fatal, whatever it is disease. Please have her not be picked up by the police, and let her graduate from high school." Pretty humble, you know, And it hasn't been all that bad. It's great that she's getting good grades and everything, that's a big plus. But I've seen a lot of unhappiness out there, so for me it starts with that basic happiness.

Barry: I'd like to see children grow up to find their values in their own livelihoods, their own gifts and skills, the people they care for.

Janet: One thing I've heard Anna say is that it's not the education that really makes the person—it's the home life. It's really that deep respect for the child's own free thinking, rather than just conformity.

5 KAREN LITFIN AND MAYA JACOBS

Karen lives in Seattle. She has one daughter, Maya, who also lives in Seattle.

Karen: Maya is ten now. She's really beginning to question me more, beginning to put more of a distance between us, beginning to have more of a critical consciousness.

For many children, the developmental tasks of adolescence— separating from your parents and developing your own identity—are prefigured by initial movement in this direction in the final few years of the second era.

Karen: When this distancing begins to happen, it's really important for parents to respond with a lot of love and understanding. I'm seeing how hard that is to do, because up until now Maya and I have been extremely bonded, extremely close. And except for when she was in that terrible twos period, which really hit when she was about three, there's been this unquestioning acceptance of what I say. That's not the case anymore, and it's hard not to take it personally, to take it as a personal rejection. It's hard to understand that it's a phase that she's in, that it's a developmental process she needs to go through. It's not a reflection on the closeness of our relationship, or her real feelings about me.

Karen clearly identifies the main challenge that parents face as their child becomes her own person. The pushing away from the parent is absolutely necessary, and it's inevitably painful emotionally, even when the parent knows intellectually that it needs to take place.

Karen: Recently Maya and I talked about this whole process, because she told me that it's very confusing to her. She doesn't know what's going on with her. She doesn't know why she's so critical of me, and she feels like she loves me more than anything in the world so why is she being critical of me? We had a long talk about how she was feeling about it. I was sensitive, of course, to my own feelings, but it hadn't ever occurred to me that this was actually hard for her, that she didn't know what was going on in her that was making her do this.

Maya displays a significant capacity for self-awareness at the age of ten. It's important to remember that a child may be self-aware and yet still act out the momentum for separation and identity formation in ways that feel harsh or cruel to the parent.

Karen: When we talked, I told her that it seemed to me that she was moving a little bit into adolescence, and that this is a really natural process. She was able to see her own behavior as something she's just going to go through, but she still felt some guilt about it. She felt that this was something that she was doing to me that was really wrong. She started crying about all this, and she felt bad about the way she was treating me. She was beginning to challenge everything. This had happened recently, in the last six weeks. So the two of us spent an hour talking about it, both of us crying in and out of it, because it was really hard for both of us. It's like we had this oneness, and it feels like we're moving into a period of more separation.

I told I her that this is not her fault. I'm very sensitive to it, but she doesn't have to feel guilty about my sensitivity. I told her that it's just that she is this beautiful soul who is evolving, and she's going through this stage right now. This is something that everybody goes through. And she's going to be a grown woman in ten years, and she's going to need to separate from me. She said, "I don't want to separate from you. I want to live with you forever. I'm going to rent the apartment downstairs, and we'll stay together for the rest of our lives."

One quality of the child's movement into and through adolescence is inconsistency. One minute Maya is mature enough to perceive her mother's emotional pain and feel compassion in response. A little bit later she regresses into an early childhood fantasy of being a part of her mother forever. In its essence, adolescence is a long second birth, with movement back and forth between growing maturity and temporary regression.

Karen: Ever since Maya was really young, she's had this very developed ethical consciousness. I have that in me, too, but I think it's been cultivated in me. I'm not sure that I was born with it in the way that she was. So she easily feels guilty about things. If she does something wrong, it's really hard for her to forgive herself for it.

When Maya was maybe a year and a half, she was speaking some, and she would take all of her baby dolls and stuffed animals and line them up all around the carpet. She would tuck them in like she was putting them all to bed. And she would go through this thing about who had more space than the others, who was getting more of her attention than the others. And she had to be perfectly fair with each of them. She doesn't have a sibling, so it's not like having to share with siblings. She had this strong feeling that everything around her had to be treated just right. This is something that she did; it was an ongoing practice that went on for years, until she was three or so.

As she got older, this became more clear. She's just very generous. She wants to share whatever she has with her friends, with me, and it seems to be her nature. I used to wonder, "Is she doing this because she's trying to get on somebody's good side or she's trying to make up for something bad that she thinks she did?" But it's not that; she just has this very magnanimous, giving nature to her. I know the psychological theories say that this generosity develops later, but from my observations of her, she had it from the beginning.

A child's expression of a quality of character at a very young age—in this case, generosity and a deep concern for equity—cannot be explained within our current developmental psychological frameworks. It can be understood, however, as a soul quality and an expression of the soul.

Karen: I am debating the issue now of Maya's schooling. She's at Alternative Elementary School #2 (AE #2, an alternative, more child-centered public school in Seattle that was created by the lobbying efforts of parents with post-modern consciousness), which offers kids more freedom than conventional public schools. But the school has a rather shallow view of freedom.

The other option, the Waldorf school, is very structured; it's does not offer kids as much freedom as the alternative school does. Maya is going into fifth grade next year. I think that she'll stay at AE #2, but I'm not completely sure that that's really the best place for her. If there were to be an opening in the Waldorf school, I wonder if that might not be better to have a more inward-looking and soul-nurturing structure rather than to have a shallow understanding of freedom. So I was thinking a lot about this freedom and discipline issue—I don't like the word discipline—but structure, I guess, structure that's more soul-nurturing like the Waldorf structure. And I think that actually might be better for her.

Maya now has more invested at the alternative school. She's got friends there that she doesn't want to leave. She's even talking about going to the regular public middle school, which in the past she really didn't want to do because she didn't want to be responding to all that peer pressure. So I'm surprised to hear her speaking that way, and I think her talking about going to that middle school is part of this distancing thing that she's doing from me.

Education is inevitably a challenge for parents grounded in the common vision. Given the complex economic and interpersonal dimensions of this issue, the choice often comes down to the best option available rather than the ideal one. This is a reality of the conditions of life in our late modernist society—and ought not be a cause for parental guilt. With consciousness, we do the best we can.

Karen: Even before I had Maya, I had been through a lot of psychotherapy and sort of just worked on myself. I really believed that some of the bad stuff that happened to me as a child had to do with this kind of understanding of children as these wayward, almost animals that needed to be tamed. So I went through this whole taming process, and I got very tamed. And I had problems later on in my life because of that. So I had decided long before I had Maya that I wouldn't approach mothering in that way, that a child comes into life with an evolved soul and has to be respected. When we think of the child as being younger than we are, it can be seen as simply an accident of time. In actuality the child may be more evolved than we are. In fact, my feeling is that it's quite likely that Maya is more evolved than I am just from my experience of her.

Karen's perception of Maya's evolution of soul is not an uncommon one with parents who are attentive to the soul qualities of their child. Sometimes though what a parent may be perceiving in a child in the first era who is raised with respect for the expression of her inner teacher is a quality of purity of being that often emerges at these ages.

Karen: That's not a preconception that I came with. I still know that I'm the parent; I'm the one who's done some spiritual exploration so I'm the one who's going to show her these things. I'm the one who's going to give her this nurturing environment, and then she'll be okay. But I actually have felt more from raising her that she is the one who shows me, in many ways, and that's been a great eye-opening experience. Certainly I think it's good to go into parenting or teaching with the understanding that this may be the case—that there's no kind of natural authority that's given to you simply because you're older.

I remember when Maya was three years old. She is very, very fiery. She's charismatic—children follow her. And I'm not that way. She's very extroverted, and she has a fiery temper. Boy, when she was three years old, she would lose her temper, and it was pretty scary. I tend to be very controlled, reserved, and this was like, well, what am I supposed to do with this? Early on, when she was maybe two and starting to go off, I would try to repress her. I would try to hold her down—not physically—but I would sometimes yell at her, try to overpower her, and none of this was working. It was all making things worse. I was basically doing a mild version of what my mother had done to me. It became clear that it wasn't working, and I felt terrible. I felt like my response to her was somehow betraying something that I was, and something that I really believed. And so I worked on my own anger, and I began to get at least the expression of it under control, and eventually even the anger itself pretty much dissipated.

I remember one time when I was with my mother and my sister and had Maya with me; she was very tired and probably hungry, too. And she had one of these terrible tantrums because she wasn't getting exactly what she wanted. So at that point I had developed this response where I would simply hold her, and she would lash out at me and sometimes scratch me and hit me, and sometimes I could even get hurt doing it. But I would still hold her, no matter what, I'd just keep holding her and holding her until she finally melted. She would cry, and we would regain our closeness. I didn't feel anger when I was doing this. I would just be very solid. I saw her as kind of flailing about and me being this container to hold her.

Karen offers a wonderful example of a parent first repeating an unhelpful parenting behavior she experienced as a child, then tuning into her own inner guidance and rejecting this repression as "betraying something that I was." With much will and work, she created her own way of keeping Maya safe while the child worked through her intense feelings. Perhaps the greatest challenge of evolutionary parenting is making conscious to ourselves the behavioral patterns we hold within from our own childhoods, keeping those we value and abandoning those we judge undesirable.

Karen: My mother and my sister were horrified by this. They yelled at me in the car. They said, "Karen, you have to stop doing that. You've got to get control over your child. You're creating a monster. By the time she's a teenager, she's going to be controlling you."

They said this in front of her, and she was hearing it all. She could understand what was going on. And then later on they took me aside at my brother's house, and they both told me what a terrible job I was doing at raising my child. That actually did really upset me, especially my sister, because she and I were very close, as close as I've ever been to anybody, and she just wasn't getting what I was doing. So that was the first real big disagreement we had ever had. I mean, when we were children we fought, but as adults we kind of saw each other as peers and saw eye to eye on mostly everything.

And that night I took my sister home and tried to explain to her what it was that I was doing. And she said, "Well, I guess we just have to disagree on this because I think you're making a great big mistake." My sister died a couple years after that, so she didn't really get to see. But I think she saw enough that she began to be convinced that the way I was raising Maya was good. But later on my mother—what she saw in Maya was very good, and she saw that my way was better than what she had done, and she felt she had made mistakes with us.

Often family members will see giving the child freedom within safe boundaries as spoiling the child. Karen chose to allow Maya to express her intense feelings of anger, and she found a way to provide safe containment for the child. At the time her mother and sister did not understand the reasons for or the implications of her choices.

Karen: Then that tumultuous period passed, by about the time Maya was four. Sometimes even after when she'd be tired, it would be hard to get her to go to sleep. So we would have big struggles around bedtime. Every now and then she's had temper tantrums since then—she does have a temper.

I believed that this hard period would pass, even when I was in it. But at the same time when you're in the middle of it, sometimes it's hard to believe.

One thing I saw right away back then—I saw that it simply wouldn't work to try to break Maya's will because she had a stronger will than I do. And that became really clear; she has a much stronger will. And I have a very strong will, so I was really quite amazed to see that.

The will of the first era child who has been given freedom is always stronger than the will of the parent. When a parent sees a child's will as the expression of her soul, this insight can reframe the parent's relationship with the child's will. **Her will is not the enemy; it is the child's soul.**

Karen: This was around the time that my own spiritual life deepened. Part of my spiritual crisis had to do with my parenting. I saw my response to Maya in these times, and I just didn't like what I saw at all. I felt that I needed to go deeper in myself to find a place of peace, because I couldn't maintain the peace that I normally had in my life when this would happen. It would trigger all kinds of stuff. And now, thinking back to the way I was raised, of course it triggered all kinds of stuff because my mother more or less did break my will. I was one of these very goody, goody children. And my father, too. I was terrified of my father. So when Maya would go through these temper tantrums and when my family was around, she would hit me and scratch me, and they felt that what I needed to do was hit her back and show her. They kept saying, "You need to show her who's boss." And I was saying, "I don't want to be a boss, I don't want to overpower her because I want her to have her power, but I want to contain it for her." I knew that what I was doing was right. In my soul I could feel that it was right. But it was so difficult when I realized that my family had this understanding of me as just being a terrible mother.

I'd had the experience in giving birth to Maya of her as an embodied soul, and I'd had that experience so concretely that I could never deny it. So I couldn't treat her as this wayward animal that needed to be tamed when she was going through these things. And when I would do that, I would see it as a response to my own old stuff rather than to the situation as it really needed it. And not just when I gave birth—she was so beautiful to watch grow. So I couldn't think of her as this thing to be repressed. I couldn't really believe that, I couldn't convince myself of it.

Karen's own fundamental inner truth gave her the clarity and the courage to parent in accordance with her own inner knowing.

****

This interview took place three years later.

Karen: Maya is 13 now, and she's in eighth grade at Billings Middle School (a small private school in Seattle). In the last two years she has really decided that she's a teenager. She's doing a lot of things to put distance between herself and me, and then she's sometimes coming back real close but more and more distance. She's really focused extremely on her friends, in particular one friend.

She's doing well in school. She's a good student. Last summer she had a big sense of doubt about being in school at all. She read *The Teenage Liberation Handbook*, and she was persuaded by it. She said, "This is it." Her best friend has been home-schooled and had read the book and recommended it to her, so part of it was that she was going along with her friend. And then when her friend decided that she didn't want to be home-schooled anymore—she wanted to go to Nathan Hale for high school—Maya decided she wants to go to Nathan Hale, too.

So I see her making a lot of decisions based upon what her friends are doing. And mostly nothing's getting her in any big trouble because she has chosen her friends pretty well.

At the beginning of the school year she did get into trouble. It's the first time it ever happened, and it was a big wake-up call for her. It was pretty minor stuff, really. But the authorities at school, the principal, found out. It's a small school—there are only 60 kids in the school—so things get out pretty quickly.

It was a wake-up call because she realized that she had done things that were against her true values because she was going along with other people. In particular she was going along with one girl, who she didn't even really like, but her friends liked this girl. So she thought that in order to be part of the crowd she had to do these things. You know, typical teenage stuff.

She just went through a period of about a week where she stayed home most of the time thinking about her life, spending a lot of time crying, writing poetry, rearranging her furniture in her room. At that point I allowed her no contact with any of her friends. Well, actually, she could talk to her one best friend, briefly. So she went into this place where she really looked at her life.

And she came back to school with a lot of gratitude towards the teacher and principal for how they had handled the situation, and with a lot of gratitude towards me for how I had been with her.

Gratitude is inherent in the consciousness of the child in the first era, because gratitude is a soul quality. When children's experience of gratitude in the first era is respected and nurtured, they continue to have access to gratitude later in childhood and even during the storms of adolescence, as evidenced by Maya in this experience.

Karen: There were people whom she had done some things to that were dishonest, and so I had her go and talk to those people. And every single person received her very openly. She had the sense of a kind of grace. People forgave her, and it was like a new start. It happened right at the beginning of the school year. When she got back into school after all these things happened, she was just like a different person. She was cheerful. Before that she had been sullen and complaining all the time and nothing was good and all the teachers sucked, which was her favorite word—things suck all the time. So she had a very good attitude.

Well, that rosiness lasted maybe a month or so. But it hasn't gone back to the same place it was before. So I think it's really good that this happened at this point because if it happened in a public school, like next year when she goes to a big school, I don't think it would have come out so well. She got a lot of individual attention. A lot of wisdom was put into the consequences, which were never designed as punishment. Every girl who was involved in this situation got different consequences. For Maya the consequences involved public service and also school service, and it turns out she's really good at that and she likes it. So it got her re-engaged in belonging to society and to people, so it was very good.

Every adolescent makes mistakes. At times the lure of the group, the intense desire to belong, overwhelms all other criteria for judgment. What do parents do with these mistakes? Karen's example illustrates the powerful impacts of simultaneously holding the teen responsible for her actions while offering access to restorative justice, not simply punishment. The week of solitude most likely helped Maya regain access to her own inner knowing, which is often so hard to find in early adolescence.

Karen: In terms of Maya's relationship with me, it had been pretty tense before that. She was at her dad's house every summer. Whenever she's at her dad's house, she comes home and she's always very grateful to have me as a mother. But that doesn't last long. There's this little honeymoon period where she comes home and then it's like, oh, Mom, you suck, and all that.

I mentioned to you that I had been involved in a relationship about a year and a half to two years ago, and that made her very jealous. She's never completely come back to that place of closeness with me, because the jealousy was so intense. It made a big gulf between us in her mind. So things that we used to do, like me reading to her at bedtime—she's kind of old for that—but I suspect if that gulf hadn't happened, she would still want me to do that sometimes.

Things like touching her—she doesn't like me to give her massages anymore. Even hugs are pretty scarce. But sometimes she still really wants a hug.

She's going through this period of putting distance between herself and me. And one of the ways she does it is through popular culture, because she knows that it is something that is alien to me. It's her way of defining herself as different from me. She used to play classical music on the flute. She dropped the flute this year, which was very sad for me because she's very talented, and she used to enjoy it. She doesn't remember that she used to enjoy it, but I remember that she did. I remember that she would pick it up and play it just for the sake of expression. Now she doesn't have that. The only mode she has for expressing herself emotionally is her poetry. She writes in a journal. So the popular culture thing— she listens to pop music now all the time on the radio. Fortunately, not loud.

In terms of clothes and that sort of thing, she hasn't gone too far in that direction. A little bit. She has pretty minimal clothes, considering her age. She hasn't gone too far in this direction, but I can see that it's sort of the direction towards popular culture.

Youth culture began in the United States in the 1950s-60s when our society first had millions of teens who were in school, not in the workplace, who had spending money, and who had access to electronic media: radio, records, and television. Each new form of youth cultural expression—Elvis Presley and early rock and roll; the Beatles and the 60's rock, sex, drugs, and politics; punk, rap and hiphop; grunge; the early anarchic Internet; and MySpace and Facebook and texting and Twitter—began as an authentic manifestation of new consciousness among young people. But in late modernist America, each form was quickly corrupted by capitalist exploitation. Anything that engages millions of teens can make somebody a lot of money.

Youth culture inevitably challenges conscious parents and requires trust, patience, empathy, and, when possible, critique.

Karen: A real obsession is with this one particular friend. She hasn't gotten heavily into boys yet, so her social focus is her very best friend, Hannah. She wants to talk to Hannah every day, and she makes tapes for Hannah at night and tells Hannah all about her day on the tapes and things like that.

I think she's following her peers, but it happens that her peers are into provocative things. So, yeah, rap music, for sure. And hip-hop. I actually don't even know who is all out there

There have been times where she's invited me into her room to listen to a song. I think the songs that she really likes are the songs by women about how hard life is. That seems to be something that resonates with her.

Maya has these ideas about me as being rigid and purist, that I'm against anything in popular culture. And I'm not really that way. So I like to let her know that I'm outside of her boxes, but not in a way that confronts her with it. So she wants to do this hiphop dance class. Fine with me. Really, I'd like to see her do ballet or jazz or something that really builds the mind-body connection a little better. But she wants to wiggle her hips and do provocative things on the dance floor. At least she's learning something about her body and so, sure, I'll go for that.

She said to me about a month ago, "Oh, Mom, I wish you could be normal." Fat chance with me. But I asked her, "What would help you feel that I was normal?"

She said, "Well, like you would never get a manicure."

So I said, "Sure, I'd get a manicure. I never have, but I would go and get a manicure with you."

And she said, "Really?" She was shocked, I would do that?

I said, "Let's go get a manicure," so we went out and got a manicure.

That seemed to satisfy her. And we both really enjoyed it. Actually,

I enjoyed it quite a lot. I think I would do it again.

Karen: *Just as Janet Lia chose to engage with activities suggested by her daughter, Karen makes a similar decision for the same reason: to nurture the connection.*

She sees me as this very defined—my whole life is about spiritual practice and ecological values and if something falls out of those very narrow perceptions that she's got in her mind, then I'm not interested in it. There is some truth to it, yeah. But it's not nearly as narrow as she thinks it is.

Adolescents often hold limited and somewhat inaccurate perceptions of their parents. So parents who act in gentle ways to violate those inaccurate perceptions can help their teen expand her perception of them as unique individuals, not just roles.

Karen: I really don't like going to malls. She'd like to hang out in malls with me a little more, I think. Really, she'd rather hang out in malls with her friends, but she'd like me to say, "Hey, Maya, let's go shopping." And we did that last week, but I can only handle it for an hour and a half. It is awful to me, it's just awful. So there are certain things about popular culture that kind of make me sick, and I can't be part of it.

Parents also need to be true to their own values and limits.

Karen: Some of my values have really become her values, and that's a problem that she has. They've become her values in ways that I wouldn't express them myself. So, for instance, my love of nature— I think it was in her already. She has this incredible love of animals, and she thinks a lot about saving wild animals who are hurt and helping animals who have been abused. She spends a lot of time thinking about these kinds of things. She and her friend Hannah are members of People for the Ethical Treatment of Animals, and they keep up.

She's mostly a vegetarian, but she will eat meat. At her dad's house they eat a lot of meat. So she's got something big to push against there. When she's with her dad, I think she really does push against his life a lot. But she's with him at Christmas and spring break and time in the summer. Not very much. But in her mind she pushes there. She spends time thinking about how stupid her father's family is, and how she would raise children differently than the way he and his wife are raising their children. She's really thinking about how to do things her own way.

At the same time it's me that she's got to push against. But I don't think she could ever smoke cigarettes. I think she would try it, but I think it just repulses her. So that's a value that I think is in her that's a value of mine that I don't think she'd go against. She wanted to dye her hair pink. We kind of talked around that, but we never really reached a decision. I said, "Yeah, I think it would be okay" after awhile. But she hasn't dyed her hair pink or done anything about it. What it really was "is Mom going to let me do this?" Now she wants to get her nose pierced, and I said it's okay. I think she was surprised.

Her friend at school wants to get her nose pierced, but her mom won't let her. So Maya is shocked that actually I'm letting her do things that her friend's mother won't let her do.

She says to me, "Mom, why can't you be more normal?" But she really needs for me to be abnormal so she can wish that I were more normal, right?

I think middle school is a really difficult time, especially for girls, and I wanted her to be spared a lot of what happens in the public school, and I think she has been.

****

Maya Jacobs at 19:

I've had a very eclectic schooling. I went to a Waldorf school for preschool and kindergarten and loved it, was totally amazed by it. My dad thought it was not the place for me and got me out and put me in a big, regular public school for first, second and third grade.

I hated it. I got along because I was a kid and I could mesh, but I really hated the school. After third grade when I had the worst teacher ever, I went to Alternative Elementary #2, which was a little different, at least. It was a big school and there were large class sizes, but I got to call my teachers by their first names and really got to know the teachers and really loved that school.

That was fourth and fifth grade. Then I went to Billings Middle School for all of middle school, which at that point had only 36 kids. Middle school's always a terrible time in life, so that was hard. I'm glad I went to a school that small because I don't know if I would have made it in a bigger school. Of course, I hated it at the time, but looking back, it was wonderful for me.

Maya offers an insight into the texture of early adolescent consciousness: sometimes the early adolescent perceive most vividly what she opposes or condemns.

Maya: Then I went to Nathan Hale High School for a year. I couldn't deal with having no contact with teachers and having no one know my name. The students there were so superficial in some strange way, and I was contemplating dropping out. I was really interested in unschooling—this idea of home schooling but without a parent running things for you. I decided to check out the Nova Project (a small, alternative public high school in Seattle, also created by the lobbying of parents and teachers with post-modern consciousness) because I was in desperate need of something else. And I was, okay, I was too lazy to actually unschool, so I said, "I guess I'll go to Nova for a year, and if I don't like I'll drop out." But I loved it, I just totally fell in love with it and became the captain of the first-ever sports team there, just really kind of blossomed. That was probably the best experience of my life. So I was there for three years and graduated a year ago in June.

When I went into 6th grade, I was still playing fantastical games with all my friends. And by seventh grade half my friends were smoking weed. It was just like this crazy, huge transition from innocence and childhood to…corruption, sort of. It was really hard. Two of my friends were expelled from the school for ridiculous things. I think we were all really, really lost. And still, we were in this little school with 12 kids in my class, so we all knew each other so well. It seemed almost like a family for awhile, which was uncomfortable, but it was also such good support. And I think if I'd gone to some giant middle school, I would have just been wandering around having no idea what was going on in myself.

Given the developmental challenges of early adolescence—a long, second birth of identity—the value of an intimate, personalized learning community is immense. Inevitably there's a tension of intimacy in such a community, yet the "good support" provides a safe and respectful environment in which teens can test and explore and grow—and make mistakes and learn from them.

Maya: Now when I got to Nova, I was ready for self-motivation. It's a school where you will not make it if you do not have a lot of self-motivation because you don't have to go to class. No one rides you. No teacher comes and says, "You're skipping class, go back to class." It's entirely your own choice, and that can be dangerous for many kids. For me, after leaving Nathan Hale I realized that I love education, I love learning, but I wanted to take it into my own hands and not be force-fed the way my seven classes a day fed it to me at Nathan Hale. So the fact that I went to Nathan Hale is what made me do so well at Nova, because I could just compare it to what I'd seen before and just never took it for granted. And it's the perfect size for high school, 280 kids. But there's still that really good personal care, and it's appropriate to be friends with your teachers. At any other high school it's really not, it seems like there's this really strong authority and submissive kind of thing going on, and Nova doesn't ever do that. I think I needed that. I was a really self-conscious, incompetent little kid when I went there, and then I let myself figure out what it's about.

Mark—he was a teacher but he's now the principal—was my mentor. He was always there for me, no matter what. I went to

India when I was in tenth grade and came back and tried to get credit for it. Mark totally encouraged me. He said, "Sit down and write everything." I ended up writing a 75-page book about it and got lots of credit for it. I applied to Lewis and Clark College in my senior year and got in. Then I deferred my admission for a year and travelled for the last year. I had this budding plan in my mind since I was like eight or nine years old. I didn't want to do the whole perfunctory college, grad school, job.

I've always had this weird, insatiable yearning for understanding, broadening my perspectives. Growing up in Seattle, you're pretty aware that you're around everyone else who believes the same thing in your life. But there are other people in the world other than Seattlites. My mom and I recycle everything we can, grow as much food as possible, and I love being around people like that. But I also really wanted to understand other things, other kinds of people. I don't think you can understand yourself without seeing the rest of the world in respect to yourself. So that was my goal for this past year.

Maya's comments display her deep grounding in post-modern consciousness and the beginnings of her extension into integral consciousness. At this point in her becoming, she accepts the values of post-modern consciousness on their own terms, without any need for distancing, even though these are essentially her mother's values. At the same time she is impelled to reach out beyond the boundaries of post-modern consciousness; this is a clear signal of the ongoing unfoldment of consciousness into integral.

Maya: I left in September of last year and travelled west to east. I was in western Europe and then India and then southeast Asia. I worked on organic farms about two-thirds of the time when I was travelling, and then the rest of the time I was just being your silly old tourist. I joined WWOOF (World Wide Opportunities on Organic Farms), and you can set up work visits on farms all over the world. It was really amazing, I'm so glad I did it.

I also went back to Auroville (an intentional community in south-eastern India) for three months, where I had visited before with my mom when she taught classes there. I first went there when I was 10. Auroville is really inspiring. And I have friends there whom I've known for nine years.

I think India has probably been a bigger influence on me just because being a 10-year old and seeing people really starving, really understanding that there's real poverty, real hardship. I remember coming back from my first trip to India and just being so shocked when my friends would throw tantrums over not getting their Lunchables or something. It's a way to never take your life for granted, I think, and that's kind of how I've always seen it. Auroville has really inspired me with their sustainability techniques. This last year, I worked with this guy who lives on probably a hundredth of the American footprint.

Being in India puts you in so much better perspective. No 10-year old can really understand that there are people actually starving. But when you've actually seen it and you really understand it, it changes you. I'm sure I'm still terribly spoiled compared to most children in India, but at least I'm aware that I'm spoiled.

Maya knows that her travel to India as a child and teen have added breadth and depth to her experience and have contributed to her education and to the evolution of her consciousness.

Maya: I'm really excited to go to college. I really do love your regular old conventional learning. I love reading books and I love being taught things. In fact, I even love lecture classes as long as I feel like I can get to know the teacher, I can get to know the students in the class.

So I'm excited to get into a little more conventional learning situation after Nova because that was so good while it lasted, but it's kind of done now. So I'm mostly just going to Lewis and Clark College because I'm really excited to go to learn.

Another sign of Maya's access to integral consciousness is the flexibility this choice of college displays. She is ready to attend a conventional college because she feels entirely in control of her own capacity to learn, regardless of the external environment.

Maya: I have no idea what I want to major in. Right now I guess I lean towards environmental sciences or possibly cultural anthropology or something like that. I know I don't want to be a business or econ major, that's about it. I really have no idea, and I'm hoping I don't have to figure that out for another two years.

My middle school years were just not fun, and I went into that like super-atheist. I hated anything that had to do with any religion, spirituality. It's all just b.s., you know. My mother never pushed spirituality on me, though she believed in it. And so I had that this rebelling stage.

Recently I've really been thinking about all of this. One of my best friends is very strongly Christian, and I never used to be able to be friends with someone who is a Christian.

Another indicator of integral consciousness: the capacity to value others who are centered at very different stages of consciousness.

Maya: I'd say—and especially in middle school, "Oh, how could you believe that?" So recently I've really started thinking about what I do believe in. Now I think that because I was raised by my mother, I have a lot of faith in general. I don't have a specific spirituality that I follow, and I'm definitely not religious. But now I feel that it's wonderful to be raised like I was, to be raised with trust and spirituality, trust in something larger. I definitely don't have the same views as my mother, at all. And I don't know if I would say even that I believe in God. In fact, I wouldn't say I believe in God, but I definitely believe in some higher force.

When I was a child, I used to love talking about God with people because my mom has always been just so willing and interested in these things. And my dad raised me Catholic, so I was kind of a little disparate there. It's definitely something that's played a pretty big role in my life.

I've always been pretty particular with the friends that I choose. I cannot be one of those people who just finds someone my own age and hangs out with them because I need someone to be with. I'd much rather be alone than do that. Because of that I have friends who really do see the world definitely not the same as me but who take the same approach as me—very interested, philosophical. We don't get the same answers, and we don't believe all the same things, but because of how we think, I can relate to them.

Having that India experience when I was so young and having this last year's experience—I really took all those little gems of wisdom that everybody from all around the world gave me. There's just something a lot more open, something broader about the way I think now. It's funny, the more questions you have answered, it seems like the more questions you have. Sometimes I do feel a little bit alone because of my international experiences and my willingness to take these different perspectives into consideration when I'm looking at my life or America and the problems that I see in the world.

Alone to some extent as well because her accessing integral consciousness takes her beyond most of her age peers.

Maya: Well, maybe alone is too harsh a word. There are times when I really want to talk to my friends about what it's like to be surrounded by intense poverty. Like when I was in Laos; it's one of the most undeveloped countries in the world, yet it's like one of the happiest countries I've ever been to. With subsistence, you grow your own food, you eat your own food, and you never starve. It's this whole global economy that really encourages starvation. I think about these kind of insights so often, and it's really not something you can comprehend until you've really seen it.

Even though I've travelled some, I've also led a very sheltered life compared to the rest of the world. I hate to say that travelling is the only way you can get these experiences because it's so bad for the environment and because it's like saying you can only attain spiritual enlightenment in a certain room, which I don't think is true. But forcing yourself to get these perspectives is a pretty strong way to do it.

I feel like we're in a really, really pivotal part of our existence. And I'm pretty skeptical, I guess, or maybe even cynical, about humans in general. You watch the news about global warming, and you say, "Good job, us, really a good way to take care of our home." But at the same time, humans are pretty amazing. I recognize that humans are the only creatures on earth that have the capacity to really destroy the planet, or to really bring it out. We can destroy cultures. Look at India, where on all the billboards are these white, blonde girls now, and it's sick. But at the same time, we made it, we did that, so we can also take it back.

Awareness of the inevitability of paradox is also a sign of integral consciousness.

Maya: I feel like I have to have this faith, but I do have this faith that though maybe we've messed up a lot, I feel like that's the only way we're ever really going to learn. And I do think we're going to learn from it. It's taking a lot for us to be snapped out of it, I guess. I think that the near-future is probably not going to look so wonderful. But the world's strong, and humans are pretty capable, and I think eventually we're going to mess it up enough where we finally realize what we've done and we'll be able to come out of it. Not only we as humans, but this whole giant ball and all the creatures on it.

For my own future, I don't know. My foreseeing can be a little negative, a little dark. Yet I do have this faith that things will go well, and I don't know if it's that some higher power will pull us out of it—I actually think that it's humans who are going to create it themselves.

A faith in the capacity of homo sapiens to continue to evolve in consciousness.

Maya: When I was four years old, my mom would ask, "What do you want to do when you grow up?" And I'd say, "I want to save the world." I'm slowly realizing that single-handedly it's not going to happen. But I really hope that I have a big influence, and I don't think I'd be content with my life if I didn't.

Ambition in the most noble sense, and responsibility.

6 ROBERT KNODLE AND NOAH KNODLE

Robert lives in Seattle. Noah was soon to move to New York City from northern California.

Robert: My son, Noah, is just turning 25. My younger son, Perry, is almost 23. I wanted to respect each of them for their individuality, not expecting them to be like me or different from me. I wanted to support their curiosities and encourage them to take risks, knowing that they were loved and trusted. I wanted to provide them with support, not just the financial support of having a home and food and clothing but emotional and intellectual support. If they had issues that they felt comfortable bringing to me, I wanted to be available. I wanted to be a model of growth and comfort with the idea of challenge.

In his own words Robert describes the common vision's emphasis on freedom within safe boundaries and love and support.

Robert: I felt that honesty with myself was the key to providing a model of integrity that I could show to them. Compassion for other people was something that I hoped to give them as a value that they could carry forward within their lives. Also, a comfort with the exploration of what spirituality can be.

I found myself being very consciously hesitant about offering them a model of spirituality, a form of spirituality to try to embrace or live into. I have questions about that as I grow older, about whether or not more form at some point would have allowed them the freedom to reject it and choose some other form, and maybe it's harder to find a form if you never had one that was clear and habitual. I had too many experiences of oppressive forms when I was a youth, so I chose to sort of err on the side of freedom. But I hope that they will be able to recognize the importance of spiritual interests and pursue them as they grow older.

Robert's stance on the role of religion in children's lives is common among parents centered in post-modern consciousness. From here the greater good is perceived as protecting the child from the harms of traditional consciousness religions. In contrast, from an integral perspective, Inayat Khan suggests that engaging the child in a religious form during the second era of childhood can be an enriching experience, because children in this era seek and value clarity and concreteness in forms of experience. He also notes that parents who make this choice need to be prepared for the child as a teen in the third era to turn around and reject this religious form, as he explores and then defines his own personal spirituality.

Robert: Noah was funny, he was energetic, he was creative. These sound like such cliches, but I remember the kind of play that he could create, all the imagination that he had.

We lived in a kind of intentional community setting here in Seattle, where there were other children Noah's age, and we had worked hard to live closely enough together that we could tear down fences and create an urban oasis for them to enjoy. So they enjoyed a lot of freedom to play outside in the yard and gardens, climb the trees. It was a safe place in that we knew where the kids were at all times, but there were trees to climb and all kinds of challenges. Noah was able to play a lot, and so he was playful. He was energetic and athletic.

Freedom for the expression of the will, within safe boundaries.

Robert: More than other kids Noah was interested in giving to other people. I often wondered if it was out of a need to satisfy other people, or a need to be recognized by other people.

Or simply a quality of his soul.

Robert: If we were off to potlucks, he wanted to bring the food. If there was gift giving to be done, he wanted to be the gift giver. I remember when he was around 5 or 6, we were walking to the store together and he saw a boy with his dog sitting by the donut shop, on the sidewalk. The boy was 13 or 14. Noah wondered if the boy was homeless, if he had anyplace to go. And it was a real strong concern on his part. I was quite surprised to hear that Noah had an awareness of homelessness at that time.

He took a great interest in compassion in relating to the people around him. He was really good with younger kids. By the time he was 4 he was good with kids who were 2. When he was 8 he would be taking care of 4-year olds in the little community. So he was always focused on being a nurturing sort of fellow.

Noah went to kindergarten, he didn't go to preschool. We had considered putting him in a Waldorf preschool-kindergarten that we had heard about. One of my friends put their son, who was Noah's nearest peer in age, in this school. But when we visited the school, I learned that this was the first step towards an eight-year commitment with one teacher. I said, "That sounds enough of a serious decision that I think I'll wait on this one." I ended up putting him in kindergarten at an alternative elementary school here in Seattle. He didn't start school until he was five and a half. He went to public school through third grade and then moved to the Waldorf school for fourth grade. By then, I had decided to put Perry in the Waldorf kindergarten because I knew it would be a more nurturing, more calm, more stable environment than the public kindergarten would have been, and my marriage was breaking up. So I became a single, full-time parent, and I need to have both boys in the same school so their schedules would match.

When Noah started out at the public school, it seemed to me that he didn't think he was as smart as the other people. He had friends whom he felt were smarter. He didn't have a high impression of himself as a reader or as a student. He had wonderful teachers, and the same teacher for kindergarten and first grade, and then another teacher for both second and third grade. The teachers liked him a lot. They thought he was very creative and artistic, and they didn't have negative things to say about him or concerns to bring. But Noah just never seemed to feel real happy about school. He enjoyed the friends that he had, but he didn't enjoy riding the bus to school.

Noah came to the Waldorf school in fourth grade, and his teacher was a very musical individual, a very, very warm, sensitive man. Noah connected with him very, very well, and he was very disappointed when that man had to leave after only one year.

Noah enjoyed being at school, the friends that he made. But my experience was that he wasn't as connected to the teacher that he had in the later years as he was to the teacher that he had that first year. He could also feel more exposed than most kids, because he stood out with his ethnicity—his mother is Filipino.

As for the Waldorf curriculum—he had some of the same troubles that other students I've observed had when it came to connecting to the instrumental music parts of the Waldorf program, but he did a good job of giving it a try and working with it. But the artistic work—the drama work, the hand work, the things that he knitted or the things that he sewed—he cared a lot about that and had a lot of fun with. He was as good a student as most, from my observation. At the end of eighth grade, he wanted to get back into the mainstream of public school. He knew that the Waldorf world was a little artificial in the sense that it was a minority philosophy. It was not what everybody else was doing, because he had some knowledge of what everybody else was doing from his friends outside of school.

So Noah went to Roosevelt High School (a large public high school in Seattle). When he went back to the public school, he went back with a mission. He was going to reconnect. He knew, I think, that kids, when they're 13, 14- years old, can make some very powerful decisions, very consciously. And the issue of what kind of person do I want to be as I step forward is one they can make with a lot of power. They may end up regretting the decisions, because they can't make them with much wisdom, but they can make them with a lot of power.

Robert describes the adolescent's desire to connect with the larger world beyond the family and to begin to make sense of that world for himself.

Robert: Noah went to Roosevelt, and he knew right away who were the cool kids, who were the competent kids, who were the kids that other people didn't like. He figured out the social structure, and he went for the top of it. He felt unrecognized as a freshman going in, that he didn't know very many people. By the end of his freshman year all of that language had stopped, and what I was hearing more was the athletics that he was participating in, the friends that he was making, his new group. As a student he was doing fine in school, and he continued to be that person like he was as a child, the one to take the food to the potluck.

By that time I had married again, and Noah found himself with a step-brother and a step-sister. So the family dynamics at the point when Noah went into high school became more complex.

Noah and I had some difficult times during his high school years. I interpreted them as him having a hard time choosing between being what he wanted to be for his friends, or being with me in a way that I had known him all his life. I mean, he was able to choose how he wanted to present himself to his friends in high school. But he and I had known each other for all these other years, and so I think he found himself a bit stuck between which kind of a person he was, who was he going to be.

This is the challenge of identity development central to unfoldment in these years of adolescence—and particularly in the early adolescent years: who am I?

Robert: Noah had some rebellious times. There were times when he didn't want to talk about what was going on with him. There were times when his anger was a challenge for him to express in a constructive manner with me. We struggled through some different therapeutic activities to try to help us communicate clearly. It's interesting that over this last Christmas break he wanted to explain that time in his life as a time when he was very unhappy with the material lifestyle that we had, compared to the friends he was trying to have. And it wasn't until he had gotten to college where he recognized what an absurd connection to that stuff he had had in high school. He had felt badly about how he had tried to hold me accountable for things that he had discovered I shouldn't have been held accountable for. But I had no clue until this Christmas that that's any of the thinking that had gone on for him over the last four years of college. That was interesting.

Noah's self-awareness at 24 allowed him to see the conflict in his teen years between his father's relative modesty in material possessions and the more expansive materialism of his upper middle class Seattle school friends. His compassion and sense of responsibility led him to express his regrets to his father.

Robert: There was a time after his freshman year in high school when he became most unhappy about the awareness I had of him in the house combined with all the complexity of living in the blended family. He ended up spending most of his sophomore year at his mother's place. He would only live with me every other weekend, where before it had been easily half time or more. Then in his junior year he came back to my house more.

Noah is always pursuing life through his relationships with people. He never approaches it as an interest in a subject, or as a physical challenge to make something. It's always expressed through his relationships with people. I didn't necessarily expect him to make the same choices that I would make. He ended up choosing to be in a fraternity in college—that was absolutely a choice that I would never have made. I supported his decision. I supported his right to make his own decision. I always had questions about the decision but I never questioned him.

Robert's respect for Noah as his own person and his trust in his son's capacity to make good decisions for himself is evident.

Robert: I watched him be involved in campus life at the University of Washington, and still I was surprised to see the level of commitment he had to finding a deep friendships that ended up demanding his involvement in lots of work. He ended up being on the Associated Students board. He could have done the stuff that he did, he could have achieved the status that he did, without getting involved in the anti-rape campaign or some of the things that he found himself getting drawn into and then working hard to support. He found that he couldn't just take the glory. There was work that came along with it, and he embraced that and did a good job of it.

He really wanted to learn how to do things, not just to be the person whose name is on the poster. He knew that what he did in college could help him later in his life in practical ways, but he also always had his compassion as a motivator. He wanted to understand how to make things happen. And it really involved, who do I meet and talk to so I can get this done, and what do they need to know? And so it was really a ton of networking on his part. Then he also got enough work done that he got his double major.

Noah has had this dynamic between compassion and self-gain. I think that he thinks that if he allows compassion to be a clearly articulated goal for everybody else in the world to see, it will be interpreted as a weakness in him. And he doesn't want to be perceived as weak. He also doesn't want to be perceived as just expressing his father's liberalism. So for him, he's got sort of a tough-ass compassion.

In high school he wrote a paper for a language arts class, and in it he created this fictional character—it was himself—who was a doctor who was going to a conference on vacation in some

Mexican resort. And while he was walking along the streets he heard some whimpering in an alley that he was walking by. He stopped and looked in, and there was a little boy there, homeless and hungry and crying. He brought him out of the alley and got some food for him and started writing him. Then when he went back to the United States he eventually adopted this young boy and brought him to the states. So it's two worlds for Noah. He wants to be a very large success, but he can't get away from his concern for the weak and under-cared-for people. So he's going to have to struggle with how can I not be weak when I pursue those goals.

According to his father's narrative, Noah has access to post-modern consciousness—and he also clearly has much ego identity in modernist consciousness, with much care for succeeding in conventional terms.

****

Noah Knodle at 25:

I went to public school first from kindergarten, Summit K-12 (an alternative, child-centered publicschool in Seattle that at the time included students from kindergarten to high school seniors), then to Waldorf school from fourth grade through eighth. Then I went to a public high school in Seattle, Roosevelt. And to the University of Washington right after that.

When I graduated, I got a job with the Gallo Winery, and I've been working down in California, San Francisco, for the last two and a half years. In two weeks I'm moving to New York for this job.

What I remember most from the Waldorf school is creativity, a huge emphasis on peers, and the strong one-on-one teacher-student relationship. I think it also opened my eyes to a lot of different cultures. There was not really one specific religion or culture that they targeted; you got to learn quite a bit about the backgrounds of absolutely every civilization and religion.

I had a very small class, usually nine kids, although it grew to 12 at one point. I got a lot of that one-on-one time with the teacher. And we got to try stuff that you wouldn't normally try in another school, such as musical instruments. The only time I've ever felt truly musically inclined was at Waldorf. I played everything from a flute and a recorder to a violin and a saxophone after that. And I think I even played the piano. You just had more of an outside, creative influence.

In terms of the actual school there's a lot more drawing and painting. Everything that I got there I'm still able to use. In high school I was able to put together some of the best reports because it wasn't just letters and words—there was a lot of the creative side that I brought forth from Waldorf.

And then in business today, when I'm doing a sales presentation, it's not cut and dry. I can actually make it a very interesting presentation and have fun with it. So that's pretty much the gist: creativity, you get to try a lot of things that you normally wouldn't do, and it's very family-oriented.

At Waldorf school I had the same teacher for the last four years. That was very significant. I can't say we had the best relationship all the time, but you do get to see a lot more of each person's personality. I feel like I learned quite a bit from my teacher.

When I first went to public high school, it was difficult at first. Not knowing anyone in that sort of social atmosphere is difficult. At that time in your life you obviously have popularity at the forefront; there's a whole call for acceptance that I think adolescence demands.

It took about a year and a half for me to put myself out there. But in the end, I was able to make friends with just about every group. I relate that back to Waldorf in the sense that I didn't really have the standards that say, okay, you're going to fit in this group. You're going to be a jock, you're going to be a hippie, you're going to be an alternative kid. I didn't see those type of boundaries the way most people did in my school. At Waldorf, even though the class was small, you're interacting all the time with kids with different backgrounds, with different strengths. And you're also interacting with younger and older kids. So you learn to know these people for who they really are, not their outside influences.

I've had friends that came out of the public schools, from sports teams or something like that on the side, who would classify people in certain groups and say, "Okay, don't talk to that guy, he's this, or don't talk to her, she's this." So I think that that aspect, just coming into a public school at 9th grade, you just don't see the same barriers or see the same social classifications that public school kids have grown up in. So at Roosevelt, I'm sure some people classified me as being in a certain group of my own. I didn't see it that way. And however people saw me, I don't think I ever took that to heart and let it affect the ability to try to build relationships with many different kinds of people. And in the end I can say that I had a really great high school experience, from the friends I still keep in touch with from high school to all the extracurriculars I was involved with.

Academically the transition had some difficulty, too. Public school is very structured. Waldorf is more wide-ranging. But I figured out the high school soon enough. And my high school teachers loved creativity. You can put together a report and still make your own drawings, do your own pictures. Or you'll have a report where a report won't have a full page of text. It will have it intertwined with maybe a picture or something that sets the scene. Waldorf really helped; my ideas were more outside the box.

I found the same situation in college. For example, in creative writing at first I thought I wasn't probably the best person for writing courses. But in working with my professors the only critique I got was that I was thinking outside the box more than any other student. I was able to analyze a scenario much differently. I don't see the typical, everyday picture, and actually I was able to excel and be one of the top students in every writing course that I took because I was able to see something different, see the creative sides, get more in depth, and have a lot more fun with the topics.

Noah credits his Waldorf school experience with giving him ready access to his creative and expressive skills. This credit is no doubt deserved, but it's likely that his father's ongoing invitation to him to exercise his own will also had much to do with this aspect of his personality.

Noah: On top of that, you use a lot more technology in college. So something like Power Point, once you understand the basics of the technology then you can start incorporating stuff that you learned at Waldorf. You know, what can make this presentation fun? What could make it different than the rest?

At Waldorf school, we used zero computers. I didn't have a computer to use at home either then. But in my generation, you learned to use computers on your own any way. They didn't have that much going on even in high school then. I also grew up without a television. I do have a little brother who's 12. And he's great at the computer, but I think it definitely puts some restraint on your ability to think.

After I graduated from the University of Washington I got a job with Gallo and moved to California. I started off as a sales representative, representing the company in Sonoma. They definitely make it very clear once you move past that sales rep role that they're definitely matching your personality with your territory. The area in Sonoma is pretty eclectic, having many different types of people: farm workers, blue collar jobs, upper middle class, and then upper class. And you've got different wines, all the way down to your economy wine drinker.

They were able to read my personality well enough through four interviews to understand that I didn't see any barriers. I could get out there and not be afraid to go off and introduce myself to any different type of person.

Noah's capacity for engaging comfortably with all kinds of people is a theme that runs throughout his young life. His generosity and compassion, which are both soul qualities, likely rest at the heart of this capacity.

Noah: Two, in sales you do need to be very creative, especially in a very high profile market where you're selling wine in wine country, and you have a million different competitors. So you're out there, they're trying to find some way to separate themselves from the competition, and it all comes down to relationship building and creativity. That's the very basis of our sales structure.

In college I was not thinking about being in the wine business. I was involved a lot in extracurricular activities, student government, all sorts of on-campus positions. I actually was working at the career fair where Gallo was recruiting new employees; that was my initial contact with them. In my new position in New York I'll be managing a sales team of six, and I'll be in charge of Queens, the Bronx and part of Long Island. In New York we have very little market share, so this is really a re-launch of our company. I'm excited to be part of it just because it is something that doesn't happen very often. How often does a company as large as Ernest and Julio Gallo get to launch a distributor in one of the top cities in our country? It's going to be very fast paced, and it's going to be probably one of the better learning experiences I've had so far.

I can relate this challenge back to Waldorf school, to the fact that once you get started in something you're going to take it head on, full force, and do something to the best of your abilities. When I was younger, I didn't see myself going into a private sector, wearing a suit and tie every day. But it's definitely grown on me; it's something I definitely love.

Down the road—I've got so many creative ideas, and I think I can start my own company doing something that I absolutely love. Obviously, sales can be stressful, but right now it's a learning experience. What I'd like to do is take the skill sets that I've learned in terms of how do you do business with clients, how to get a product in distribution, how to market something. I'd like to run my own small company. I'd like to get creative and build new things, new devices to help better different industries. I can't say for sure I'm going to better society in terms of what I'm going to do in my business career down the road, although I can try. But I can make sure that I am helping out in some way. I've always volunteered, even in high school, in college, and now in my professional career, giving back to society in some form or another. In San Francisco I've volunteered to help homeless people. One time I bought $180 worth of pizza and gave it to homeless people. So when I move to New York, I'm sure I'll do some kind of volunteering as well.

Noah wants to succeed within the terms of modernist consciousness in our modernist, capitalist society—and given his access to post-modern consciousness, he also wishes to continue his lifelong commitment to compassion, generosity, and caring for others. The avenue he seems most likely to pursue is one some have called "conscious capitalism."

7 ROBERT GILMAN AND CELESTE GILMAN

Robert lives in a small town on Whidbey Island not far from Seattle. Celeste lives in Seattle.

Robert: I'm actually in quite a bit of communication these days with both my 31-year old son, Ian, and my 21-year old daughter, Celeste. I think that [my ideas about parenting] evolved. A lot of it was just out of my own family background. But it wasn't as if it was all clear to me when we started out. I can articulate more of a perspective now certainly than I could have then.

There was very much of a sense that the child was a person, and to be respected as their own person and by no means a blank slate. And that our role as parents was to help with the coming out, the sort of nurturing forth of the potential that was there. But it was a dialogue with the potential that was there; it was not simply something that we imposed.

Robert captures the essence of the common vision in this description of the relationship between the child's nature—the potential inherent—and her nurture: a dialogue.

Robert: I would describe the child's person on a variety of different levels. First with the sense that there is a certain being-ness that is there with each person that includes as part of it a particular calling, a certain life agenda. I like to say we have at least eight billion soul stories on this planet. So it's not that there is some generalized abstract notion of what the good life is, because for each person living what they incarnated for is a very unique story.

The soul incarnates with an inherent calling or purpose.

Robert: There were a couple of things that I think were fairly consistent approaches for us. One was that even for young children, children below the age of seven, where various people would say that they don't have all of the reasoning ability or whatever, we would still always try to communicate what was the principle behind our parental saying this and not that. Because we certainly did set parental boundaries and guidelines. And where possible, without being too far out with this, we would try to make it so there was some way for the child to experience the consequences so that it wasn't just a matter of our word. But it was a matter of something where it was experienced, and then we could refer back to that and reinforce it.

Very early on we encouraged the sense that there are some ways in which the world simply works. There are some rules that you may choose not to follow, but there are reasons why there are rules and they make sense. And actually you can probably accomplish what you really want to accomplish if you learn how to use those rules well. So there was certainly an encouragement of a sense of orderliness and a sense of where the issues were. There was some flexibility, and then there are places where it is just gravity—and you don't have a lot of choice around gravity.

Robert's articulation of the idea that "there are some ways in which the world simply works" is an assertion of appropriate boundaries for his children.

Robert: I think that led to an encouragement of a certain orderliness and a sense of a discernment that helped to eliminate a lot of the rebellion issues. Because when we communicated that this is the way things work, it wasn't a power struggle between us and the child. It was more we have this additional experience, so let us show you that there's something that needs to be paid attention to here. And at the same time encouraging them to take on as much responsibility as they could handle along the way, and frequently actually letting them know that there was more responsibility available to them.

So within those boundaries, much freedom—and sometimes, more potential freedom than the child was ready to assume in that moment, so she perceived a quality of openness in her life.

Robert: What both kids often did say was, "Well, actually, we appreciate having the parental support or parental assistance." And we essentially said, "Look, we're happy to provide this support and assistance, but also you know that we're not the ones that are holding you. This is your choice, and as you want to move further out, we will assist in your moving further out."

In this way, Robert and Diane, his wife, invited their children to express their will and experience freedom while providing the assurance of support along the way.

Robert: Celeste is very consistent. Ian is consistent, too, but Celeste is even more so. There's just the sense of this continuity of person. I don't know whether Celeste told you the story about how Diane had this strong sense of Celeste's presence before she was conceived, even dialoguing with her. Diane had the sense of who she was at that point, which was consistent with who she was as a child. And so it's been right on through, from before conception on to the present.

Celeste is just an unusual person, yes. But we related to both of our children as if they were extraordinary. Not in a glamorized sense, but we allowed for that possibility. We looked for it in a certain sense, or we were open to it. Yet the extraordinariness that is there in every person is most likely to get a chance to blossom when the parents are seeing their role as assisting in the blossoming of this flower that already knows what it looks like when it blooms. And it can either be a really healthy bloom, or it can be a wounded bloom.

If every human birth is the joining of soul and flesh, then every human is indeed unique, literally unique. This is what Robert means by the word "extraordinary" in this context. What if every parent viewed her newborn child as possessed of her unique, "extraordinary" potentials that could unfold with appropriate nurture and love? Celeste may well be extraordinary in her being and qualities—and/or her expression of this being and these qualities may have been evoked, to a lesser or greater extent, by her parents' perception of her extraordinariness.

Robert: I love the Tibetan sense that when a child is born, they greet the child as welcoming back into the family. So that combination of recognition that this is a young child, doesn't know how to handle its body yet, a lot of the rules of the game that it doesn't know. So there's this really clear parental protection in assisting development and guideline-setting and all that sort of thing on the one hand. But on the other hand, here is this very honorable being, who knows its own story and knows its own blossoming, what it's moving towards, better than anyone else can ever know. And so it's that respect for knowing that I think has been really important. At the same time, there's the parental awareness of the need for playing an appropriate parental role for issues that any child will need to deal with.

This very honorable being who knows its own story.

Robert: It really does make sense to provide the child with an appropriately rich environment. I don't mean monetarily rich, but information, experience, stimulation rich. You can take it too far, but something where the child is not held back in their own exploration and development in that sense. Just make sure that the trough has adequate water. You don't have to plunge the horse's nose into it. Once you've made sure there's a nutrient-rich environment, just let the growth process that's coming out from inside the child move in its own way.

As Maria Montessori said, follow the child.

Robert: Both of my children didn't actually learn to read until they were about seven. It certainly hasn't held them back in the least, and since they learned to read, they've been readers! We did a lot of reading to them, and there was a lot of conversation in the family. So their verbal skills were well developed. And both of them were in public school as part of that. We treated school as a resource. We were not ideological about saying, "We're doing home schooling, absolutely no public school." We felt it was actually very useful after the first five years at home for them to get some time in kindergarten, first grade, second grade, when it seemed to be just a very useful step. And when they returned to home schooling after that, they knew what school was.

We were fairly careful not to set up "forbidden fruit" situations. So while we had relatively minimal TV watching in the family, TV was not taboo. They always experienced it. And in the same way, public school was not taboo.

I was really influenced by John Holt and his notion that the issue is not the kind of school; the issue is school. And it never made a compelling case for us to try Montessori or Waldorf. In fact, in some ways it made more sense for us to do the generic public school. So our kids really had the more common experience.

Not to say that both Waldorf and Montessori and other settings may not work really well. I just say whatever your options are out there, just treat them as elements in a tool box, and make sure that one of the elements in the tool box is always not school.

Robert's approach to the question of his children's education includes two elements: inviting his children to experience multiple learning environments, and respecting his children's decisions about which learning environment is best at every given age. So the children went to school when they wanted to go—and they had access to home education when they wanted to leave school.

Robert: Here on Whidbey Island, the high school is set up so that homeschoolers can do it cafeteria style, just select individual courses. And that's what Celeste did. Then she did her GED and was admitted to Evergreen [State College} with an academic scholarship.

There was one time where setting some limits with Ian, I spanked him. It wasn't great physical abuse, but it was a whack. It definitely got his attention, and it seemed to serve its role. I know it's not politically correct at this point, but it was one of those times where that was finding the right way. So, I think it was [the right choice]. It was really just something where he was pushing in a way that we needed to communicate to him that we are serious.

As much as one wants to look at the soul aspect, children are also very human, and they bring all the complexities and difficulties and paradoxes of that humanness. And so I think it's important to be light on yourself as a parent. An important part of the modeling that you need to do for the child is that you honor your own needs as well. And without taking this to the point of just being a copout, there are ways in which because you recognize the responsibility of the child for their own life, the fundamental responsibility that this being has for its own life, that shifts some of the burden off you. You do what you can, obviously with as much love as you can, but their life is up to them, not up to you. I think this is an important realization.

To be the parent you want to be, you need to allow yourself your mistakes and failures—and learn from them. As Robert says, to "be light on yourself."

Robert captures the paradoxical core of parenting: what you do matters so much for your child, and inevitably your child is her own person, with her own path.

Robert: In those first few years the child is struggling with the way in which they still have a fair bit of connection to their soul-level existence. They're struggling with how does it really work here in the body. The parents tend to be really interested in getting them to understand the constraints and limits -- don't run out in the road, don't jump out windows -- all of which are really good parental things to communicate. However, in the process of doing that, if more parents could communicate the delicate balance between the material and the soul—don't lose your soul connection at the same time that you learn to understand the constraints of the physical. Understanding this is way more important in the first few years of life than something like learning to read or any of the kind of outward skills.

Robert's assertion is coherent with the common vision's description of what serves the child best in the first era of childhood: to be invited and allowed to live in the world of her imagination, which is the realm of her soul.

Robert: With the patterns that both my kids went through, what they learned was largely what was interesting to them. We trusted them in learning what was interesting to them, although it didn't follow the standard curriculum. Yet whenever they were tested relative to the standard curriculum, they did remarkably well. So I would say for parents to just be very relaxed. If your kids are interested in their lives, then they're likely learning what they really need to learn. And even if they wind up being behind in some particular area, their "learning how to learn" skills will be so good that they'll just catch right up.

Focus on how well is the child is developing these fundamentals of being able to integrate soul and physical, and the learning how to learn skills. If all of that is going well, the academic side of things is just not going to be a problem.

Curiosity, interest, and engagement are all manifestations of the child's will, which is the inner teacher. Follow the child, trust the child.

****

Celeste Gilman at 17:

With my particular life I've had a number of years of personal challenges, and because of that I've been learning a lot and growing a lot in a sort of personal way, but I haven't been able to necessarily focus on academics quite as much.

I study what I'm interested in and what I think would be valuable for me in my life to know. And I've gone about that with everything from taking classes at the local high school to reading books to doing math from textbooks and watching videos and talking with my father or other people.

I went to public school for first grade, second grade, fourth grade, and fifth grade, and the first half of sixth grade. And then in sixth grade I was just terribly bored. I was not happy with the social situation, I was getting backaches from all the books I was carrying, and it just wasn't working for me. So that's when I decided to homeschool. I did a correspondence course for awhile. But that didn't work for me, either, because it didn't have advantages of a classroom setting, of learning from teachers and the other students, and it didn't have the advantages of self-direction because somebody else was telling me what to do.

So next I went to just doing my own thing. I created the structure. My parents were there to support me whenever I had any question or concern or anything. That's when I was in sixth grade. And on the whole, I've been very happy with it. I feel good about who I am as a person. When I do dip back into the world of high school a little bit, I don't feel like I've missed out. I've taken some high school classes, and it's been just fine socially and it's given me an opportunity to see what school is like. Something that I've noticed when I have attended classes at the high school is the difference between the way students act in elective classes and the way they act in required classes. In elective classes they're just so much, for the most part, much more focused and enthusiastic, and a lot more is able to be learned.

For the past six years I have been a self-directed homeschooler. This has served me well, allowing me to become adept at learning to learn as well as supporting my study of conventional and unconventional subjects. My homeschooling has also made it possible for me to take advantage of unusual circumstances in my life, such as travel.

Through my middle and high school years I was given complete freedom to study what I wanted. With freedom comes responsibility, a fact I took seriously. I knew my educational choices would affect my future profoundly. With this understanding I was willing to persevere through subjects I found less than thrilling. However I rarely had to apply self-discipline to get myself to study. I find the world a fascinating place and understanding it better is a pleasure for me.

In my education I have followed a variety of learning strategies. These have anchored in me a proficiency in gaining knowledge and skills through diverse means. For some subjects, such as math and astrophysics, I used a text and the assistance of an experienced adult. Much of my learning, however, has been eclectic and cumulative. For example, my curiosity would lead me to ask my father to explain why the color of the sky changed at different times of day, or I would learn about Roman life while visiting Pompeii in Italy. In this sort of situation what I was learning did not fit into a larger course I was taking. Yet because I was interested in the information, I remembered it. Then when I encountered a related bit of knowledge days, weeks or months later, it connected with what I already knew, building my overall understanding. Particularly in this sort of piece-by-piece learning, I drew on many sources of information, such as books, people, computer programs, museums, informational television, CDs, the internet, and direct observation. I am very comfortable seeking out new information.

This ability also benefited me in more structured learning situations. One of the resources I used for my education was the local public high school. I took a total of seven classes there over two years. In addition to the skills and content I learned, I feel that it was valuable for me to experience education in a conventional setting. While I was engaged in my self-studies, I felt very content with them, but I did not have the means to judge my progress compared to the average. At school I found I performed well academically (I have a 4.0 for the classes I took there) and that my will to learn meant that I enjoyed and gained more from the courses than most of the other students.

Directing my own education has allowed me to study subjects that are rarely, if ever, offered at conventional high schools. Most of these are subjects that I have been exposed to because of my parents' work as sustainability catalysts (www.context.org). Among other things, their work has involved a great deal of travel, much of which I was included in. In all I have been to 19 countries on 5 continents, spending about a sixth of my life outside of North America. In these travels I have visited many places that are developing and utilizing ecological building, biological wastewater treatment, appropriate technology, and sustainable agriculture.

In addition to the specific technologies and techniques that I have learned from these travels, they have also shaped my way of thinking about the world. They have helped me to be aware of the interconnectedness of life. I feel that if one looks at an object out of context, one is not truly seeing it. If a pest is ravaging a crop, it is not because the pest is too abundant per se; it is because there is an imbalance in the ecology that allows the pest to proliferate. This sort of thinking is about looking at systems and dynamics, and its practical application involves working with, rather than against, nature. Studying more sustainable ways of meeting human needs is important to me, as I intend to be a facilitator of ecologically and socially responsible design in the built environment.

I'm thinking of starting college in the fall of next year. I'm still in the stages of assembling a list of schools and I haven't been pruning it down yet. But I'm interested in the built environment and how the built environment can be best designed to serve all the many needs of people and be in harmony with the natural world. So I want a school that's going to help me learn about that.

There's something I've been realizing about my education. The key thing is not the way I've done my education. It's not the details of how I've learned things, but the philosophy that each child has her own unique life path. Each person has their own unique path, and nobody can know better than them what is appropriate for them to learn. And so I think that, regardless of the setting, that that's appropriate for all people. I know this by looking at the world and seeing how many different lives there are, and what a huge, vast pool of knowledge there is. And each of those lives draws on different parts of knowledge.

It also comes from my spiritual perspective of seeing people as embodied souls. We don't know what our life path is going to be consciously, nor do other people know for us. And so if in that whole mix there is anyone who can have any inkling of what the appropriate learnings for this life path are, it would be the unconscious, or the consciousness, through the impulses of the person on that path.

My spiritual life is something that I can say I've concentrated on a lot in the past six years. I've just developed—through the difficulties that I've gone through and some of the books and things that my family has been exposed to—a way of looking at the world, looking at the world and imagining things from the soul's perspective. And it's amazing. I went with some friends to see a musical on Eleanor Roosevelt, and it was really interesting for me to watch. Eleanor Roosevelt was married to FDR, and then FDR has an affair with Lucy what's her name, and Eleanor had been frustrated because she wasn't going out and doing her work in the world that she'd wanted to. And this seeming tragedy of the affair was what broke her out of her rut, and she decided that she would go and work in the world. Then Franklin got struck with polio, and another tragedy was what really got Eleanor out doing things in the world. Just seeing how these human difficulties were really enabling that person to do what she came here to do, and to do work in the world. The world looks so much different looking at it from that perspective.

As for me, there's a lot that I don't know yet, and, of course, that's natural. But I do feel that it's a life of service. I do feel that. I don't feel that I'm here to just go through my own growth things. I feel like the difficulties of my past six years have been to help me to grow and learn and understand so that I can be of greater service. And I still don't know how I'm to be of service, but that's really the way I see it.

I feel a sense of frustration and fear about what's going on in the world now. It's just really been coming home to me on a different level the horrible things that happen in the world, that people are actually capable of atrocious things. And while I've known about them for a long time, it's just now sinking in in a really deep way. But also I have the feeling that there's no hope unless we act in hope, and I have a determination to act with hope.

I have a great deal of excitement about the potentials. I think there are so many wonderful things that can be done, and I find that very exciting. I feel very blessed to have grown up in the family that I did and to be exposed to so many of those wonderful things.

When I think of those atrocious things people do, part of me just thinks I don't understand how they can do it. But another part of me can see how people can be pushed and just sort of lose control of themselves. Human emotions can be tremendously powerful. The struggle within ourselves can be tremendously powerful. If we have our own demons on the inside of our eyes and we look out and someone else is caught behind that, then I can see how people can do horrible things to them, but seeing them as their own demons, just not realizing it.

And then, like in the Middle East, it's these old stories of generations and generations of pain and strife. I almost wonder if there's some sort of dynamic in the culture, and even in the land, that these people are just sort of stuck in. It's hard to break out of that. It really takes a force of will.

I see two major trends in my peers. I both see an awareness and a sensitivity—an awareness of the environmental problems and social problems, and a sensitivity to other people that delights me and sometimes even surprises me. Then I also see heavy consumerism and just so many people largely lost in that world and not seeing the bigger picture, the bigger concerns.

I think that somehow there needs to be a way for teenagers to have something special about teenhood other than sex and drugs and rock 'n roll. We aren't children anymore, and we aren't yet adults. But to find a healthy middle way—I've really enjoyed times when I've worked in sort of an internship, volunteer, mentorship kind of way, to be able to help out, be of service, but also be learning and be amongst people and adults that I admire. One time was when I helped out with the preparation for an eco-village training, and then I participated in that.

Celeste understands from her own experience the capacity of adolescents to offer insight, energy, and creativity to adult society— new perspectives and new creativity—and how valuable it is to teens to be included in the adult world as valued contributors. Without having read Margaret Mead's argument on this point, she creates the same understanding from her own experience.

Celeste: I think that public schools now are going the opposite direction from where they should be going. There are so many different life stories, and maybe there is a common base of knowledge people need. I think it's true that everyone should know how to read and write and how to do a certain amount of math. But beyond that, there's such a huge field of learning, and so many different life stories. It seems like a situation setting itself up for an explosion out. Maybe [what's happening in the wrong direction] is a positive step because it will make school bad enough that people will know it has to change.

So many adults in our culture don't trust children to be interested in learning. They think that it has to be forced into them. I think that's the perspective that's present in the schools. Children are very open and intelligent, and they think, oh, this is the way I'm supposed to be; okay, I'll fight against learning, just like you want me to. So that reinforces the adults' thinking that children don't like to learn. But I love to learn, and I think that for other children who haven't had it forced out of them, they also love to learn. Learning is fascinating, the world is fascinating. There's just so much out there. And I think it's really sad, those students who don't like to learn, because it just closes down their world so much. But that's why people are skeptical about the sort of education I've done because they're afraid that I won't have the will or the discipline to learn and better myself. And at times I haven't. But when I haven't had the will or the discipline to focus on strictly academic things, then I've been learning other things.

I feel one of the definite benefits of the education that I've had is that it has really allowed me to grow in all the different levels of my being. It has allowed me to develop my spiritual understanding of the world. It has allowed me to develop really healthy interpersonal skills. It has allowed me to really be comfortable with myself, comfortable both with the things that I like about myself and the things that I don't like so much about myself, and to get to know myself very well. It has allowed me to do the academic things and study and to learn in many different ways so that I can learn about what works best for me.

I do see my life as being unusual, and I feel very blessed. I see that part of the exceptionalness comes from the start, the foundation of my parents and their working at home, and their work. And then part of it has developed with my home school, the characteristics of myself that make my education work very well for me. I've been quite happy with the social situation that I've had, but some children would like to have more interaction with their peers. Still I maintain that I think every child knows best what is appropriate for them to learn in their life, and that it's very, very important for children to be exposed to a wide range of things. And that feeling frustrated at not knowing something is a valuable tool for encouraging one to learn. I think that's much more valuable than being told that you should learn it.

I think that it's worth trying out new things, too. If you're interested in something, give it a try, and mistakes are fine. You learn from mistakes. Mistakes are being made all the time, and then being transformed into something positive. So if you're not making mistakes, you're not trying hard enough.

Dance has just been a normal part of my life. My mother was a dancer, and she would put on music and dance around the house, and I would dance with her. It's just always been there as a way of being with people, of being with myself, of expressing emotions.

I've done folk dancing and things like that. Whenever I'm in a situation where dance is being taught, I take the opportunity to learn something. I really love to swing dance; that's sort of the set form of dance that I know how to do and really enjoy. I took a ballet class when I was really little, and a jazz class when I was a little older. I didn't attend the whole class because we were doing all these plies, all these little things—we weren't really moving! I wanted to move to the music, and we weren't. Then I was in three shows, a musical and two song and dance reviews, which included learning a lot of dance steps and doing a lot of dancing.

As long as I can remember, I wanted to do theater. I'm not quite sure where it came from. My brother, who's ten years older than me, was active in theater, so maybe that was what inspired me. But we traveled a lot, and I just didn't make it happen. I did skits and things, but didn't really get involved. Then when we moved to Whidbey Island, I said, "Well, now I'm here in this place, I want to do theater." So I noticed a sign for the Children's Theatre, and I found out who ran it. I called her up and said, "Do you have anything on at the moment, can I audition?" I got a role, and that was it. I just kept going and going. That was around the time when my mother was ill. I kept doing theater projects, but they weren't feeding me as much anymore. I realized that that had come to completion, that I didn't need that anymore. So that's sort of behind me.

What I got from that was first simply the fact of wanting to do something and going out and making it happen. That was a really positive thing for me to experience. And then also being up on stage and in front of an audience and finding that I didn't have stage fright. It was a natural thing for me to do. And having that commitment of needing to go for the rehearsals and interacting with my peers. The whole experience of having something that I was interested in and really going for it, just immersing myself in it completely, thinking that it might be a possible career, and then coming to a place where I realized, oh, I'm done with this, and to let it go and not stay attached to it.

I grew up with gardening as part of my environment and something that I could participate in freely, but I didn't have any obligations around. Then when my mother died, I took on this garden here, and the whole thing was my responsibility. I started out with a great deal of enthusiasm, but by the end of a season I was feeling overburdened, because I tried to take on too much. So I sort of pulled back from it and kind of shied away. And then over the past months I've been going through sort of a healing process around that, and it's been highlighting a general tendency of mine to take on everything, instead of starting one piece at a time. I've been learning more about permaculture and been building up my knowledge base. Now I feel like I'm beginning to come full circle and I'm ready to go out and work in the garden again.

I would love to see a world in which people cease to see that there is a separation between us and the rest of the natural world. There's so much knowledge—millions, billions of years of evolutionary knowledge in nature—that we can learn from nature, and we can fulfill many of our human needs in ways that are in harmony with nature and not working against nature. So I would love to. I want to help work towards a world where humans and nature work in partnership.

I have an interest in the built environment, in the built and the natural environment. I feel that so often the human structures, the roads and the houses, are put onto the land arbitrarily. They are set, and then nature is expected to adjust to them. I really think it should be the other way around.

All of the religions that I've experienced have had a spiritual feeling to them, and I feel I've learned things from all of those wisdom traditions. In my experience of the Christian church the teachings of love of Jesus and then the sense of family and the congregation are some of the jewels for me. And then in what I've learned of the Buddhist traditions, things like having a stillness within and feeling compassion towards others and nonattachment. I notice in the milieu that I'm a part of, many things that I consider to be Buddhist often come up and seem to be a definite ring of truth in there. And then with the Sufi experience—it was really very valuable for me because I discovered that this connects in with the dance. Dance is a form that works very well for me for letting go of the mind and connecting with the deeper spirit that mind often sort of jabbers in front of. I've had some experiences with pagan celebrations. They've been very earthy and sort of a home-brew, down-to-earth, let's celebrate, which I've also really appreciated.

At the same time I don't think I ever will become a follower of any of these traditions. I have a very definite sense, expanding, growing sense of my own spirituality, and I feel that there is much that I can learn from all the wisdom traditions, but that none of them holds all the truths for me.

Next Friday is my birthday, yes. 18. I have had many challenges, many large challenges in my life over the past four, five years, and I have now come to a point where I've seen how great the gifts in those challenges were. I feel like this time is really coming to a close. It's wrapping up. While there certainly will be more challenges in my life, I now have tools that will help me to deal with them in a whole new way. I also have a sense of my plans for my future. I don't know if I've ever had as much of a sense before. It feels like a significant time, and it really does feel to me like a marking of that transition, that long, shallow transition from childhood to adulthood.

I have this vision of what I want to do in my life. It is my intent to be a fully engaged human being, and that means meeting challenges, having challenges, going to the places where it's difficult and working through those difficulties. Sometimes I have doubts, but my rationalization is that if there's something that I want to do—well, nothing ventured, nothing gained. If there's something that I want to do that I feel called to do, the least I can do is to try it, and so far I haven't been disappointed. If I've tried it, the things have come through for me to be able to do it.

I was riding the bus one day, and I was talking with a woman who was thinking about homeschooling her children. She was talking about the social situation in school. It was quite difficult, and it was sort of hardening her children. She was concerned that if she took them out of school, they wouldn't be able to cope later on in a difficult social situation. My feeling is that it's much better to have yourself in a comfortable environment where you're sure within yourself at a younger age; then when you're older, you'll have more skills to go out and learn how to deal in more challenging social situations. That's my feeling.

Childhood is a special time. It's a unique time where you're mostly free of responsibilities. As I'm sort of going beyond it, I just appreciate how precious it is. It's just very precious.

In a way the biggest accomplishment of my life so far was helping to care for my mother in her last months and being able to find gifts amongst the pain of her passing. The skills and philosophies I developed as a homeschooler—research, time management, self-discipline, communication, and taking every life experience as an opportunity for learning–proved invaluable in this difficult time.

A few years ago my mother was suddenly diagnosed with brain cancer. Two days after the initial MRI scan she had a lemon sized tumor removed. All of the experts told us that she was likely to live for only a few months. With the blindness of love, my father and I held onto the hope of her recovering. Both my father and I researched everything we could to help my mother heal. I became the family cook and read up on what foods most facilitated healing and health. My mother took dozens of vitamins each day. We also tried out many alternative healing practices.

A lot of my father's and my time was taken up simply looking after the basics of living for my increasingly incapacitated mother. At first there was just preparing meals, making sure she got her vitamins and taking her to doctors. Then there was changing her incontinence pants, cleaning up when she vomited, and helping her bathe.

My mother died six months after her surgery. The night before she passed away, I remember feeling how cold her feet were as my father and I cared for her before bed. I didn't think of it at the time, but now I wonder if the life was already leaving her body. In a way it had been for a while. She hadn't spoken for at least a week before she died. Well before she took her last breath, she had in a sense left the land of the living.

While my mother was still alive, all of my energy was focused on helping her and the hope that she would get better. With her death these became irrelevant. Gradually all the emotions from losing her began to come to the surface. Somehow I had to come to terms with the fact that my mother was gone forever. Two years later I still cry, but I have learned to draw strength from the experience of my mother's passing instead of being held back by it.

I give thanks for the beautiful relationship my mother and I had. In the sixteen years we spent together, she taught me many things which will serve me my whole life. My children will never meet their grandmother, but they will know her through the passion for living she instilled in me. My mother's death has given me a real sense of my own mortality. I have an unquestionable conviction that mine is to be a life of service to the world. There is a purpose that I wish to fulfill before I too pass along. The power of superficial pleasures and pains over me is very weak. This is not to say that I never get caught up in silly human problems or have carefree moments. I do. But always beneath it all my direction is clear. When my death comes, so be it. I just want to be able to look back and feel that I used my precious time here on this planet wisely.

Even as my mother lost her ability to care for herself and eventually passed away, she was helping me to grow. Through the process I discovered a strength within myself to do what needed to be done without complaint. I found that I was big enough to grieve my loss and celebrate the gifts in my life at the same time. I came to hold this experience of life as sacred, living with a savoring intensity and an awareness of the legacy I will leave when my time on earth is done.

So far in her life Celeste has lived the common vision, and she well understands its meanings and implications.

8 FRAN DUNLAP AND BEN DUNLAP

Ben lives in Seattle. Fran passed away in 2015.

Fran: My husband and I came to Seattle in 1979, and we met a number of people who were trying to start a Waldorf school here. I got involved, because it just seemed the natural thing to do. A lot of it just seemed to resonate with me. It wasn't that I went through any great catharsis or had to search around. It was just kind of like the angels: we got here and the school started and we got involved in it and it seemed a place that the children could be. We did lots of volunteer work for the school for all eight years. My key idea was to expose the children to not have rigid ways of doing things but to look for natural experiences, where there was a lot of energy flowing around.

Fran wanted to give freedom to her children.

Fran: We also wanted to keep them away from disruptions. We had a felt sense for the children's natures and for nurturing situations. Family meals were important. And we sang together. In the evening we tried to tidy the house so that when they would wake, they would have a new space to come into in a new day. We wanted things to be orderly around them.

Both children (Ben has an older sister) went to the Waldorf school for kindergarten through eighth grade. I wanted continuity for my children, a school where they were really nurtured. I felt safe when I left them there, that their inner core wasn't going to be damaged by any harsh kind of thing. And I trusted the teachers. It always felt good to leave them at the school. We could have sent them to a Waldorf high school, but they wanted to go to a public school by then. So they both went to Roosevelt High School (a large public high school in Seattle). My daughter now says that she wishes she had gone to a Waldorf high school. But I think it was good that they got out in the larger world then. They got more understanding and met all different kinds of people.

Fran's insight is coherent with the common vision: children need protection during the first and second eras from many elements of the mainstream modernist culture; but children who have been well protected are usually ready as teens to experience the larger world of mainstream schooling and youth culture, to gain from it when possible but also to critique it as necessary and employ good judgment much or most of the time.

Fran: My parents were Quakers. I brought a lot of that heritage to my parenting. When I was married, we started out at Quaker meeting. But we didn't have a regular attendance, so we didn't find a church home. We're very religious as far as feeling about the Spirit and light in each one. That really lives in me. I think it lives in the children, too.

To me it felt like our home life and the school life flowed into the other. I felt very happy my children were getting the fables in school, and they were getting history through some of the biblical stories and the plays that they did. So it felt very rich. There was the respect for the individual at school, and there was a strong community.

The school life also enriched our home life, since it helped to give the kids an inner stability. They are both quite modest people. I think that grows out of looking after the group rather than each person being only for yourself. A guidance counselor at Roosevelt told me once that all the Waldorf school kids they'd known were empowered and willing to take charge. I see all of this in my children's lives now—the caring for others and the willingness to do something about it.

These qualities woven together are a clear marker of post-modern consciousness.

Fran: Both Ben and my daughter have this need to heal the earth. My daughter just finished law school, and she's thinking about doing environmental law. Ben just a got a new job. He's thrilled. It's an environmental education program in an elementary school.

I believe that children are capable of so much more than we give them credit for these days. In the past they had to do a lot of work and were busy all the time. They learned they could run the plow, they learned they could make the applesauce, and they could move things. That gave them a sense of pride in learning how to do things.

Waldorf education gives kids a lot of that experience of learning how to do real things. My children always felt happy when they'd sit by themselves and draw. Both kids are fantastic artists. Ben's lettering is exquisite. So what they got in Waldorf was a lot more resources inside themselves, right from an early age.

****

Ben Dunlap at 24:

I grew up in Seattle. I started at the Waldorf school when I was six, went for nine years, and then went to Roosevelt High School. I started Waldorf in kindergarten.

What happened was this: my mom said, "Okay, you're going to kindergarten today, you're going to go check it out." Actually, this was when I was about five. We went for a visit, and I had a fairly good time there that day. Half a year later, she takes me to the first day of kindergarten for that year so I could start school. We drove in the parking lot, and I really didn't want to go. I remember being pretty scared of the situation, I think socially mostly. Or it was just kind of a fear of losing something, the life I'd had at home: my friends on my block, my neighborhood, and playing. So we worked out a deal where if I didn't want to go this year, I had to go next year. And that's how it happened.

Spoiling the child, acceding to his whims...or choosing to discern and respect the child's own deep knowing. Fran perceived Ben's reluctance to start kindergarten as developmental wisdom and chose to respect it.

Ben: I have an older sister who was in school. My mom was home with me that year. When I did go to kindergarten, what I remember now most is the social organization of what goes on in a Waldorf kindergarten. It was a very fun, creative time, with new friends and teachers that I liked, and doing lots interesting things.

When he was ready to go, Ben was happy to be there.

Ben: For example, we made paper. We got leaves and various fibrous plants and tore up shreds of either newsprint or other coarse paper. We made pulp with this paper, put it on screens, dried it out, put our leaves on it, and made our own paper. So a lot of what I remember is this kind of activity. After kindergarten the first teacher I had was a disciplinarian. The second teacher I had was much better. He was more interested in talking to students, hearing what they had to say.

When I went to high school, it was fairly overwhelming at first. The Waldorf school had about 175 students. Roosevelt had 1800. My first year at Roosevelt was socially alienating. Fortunately, I had a few friends who were going to Roosevelt whom I knew from Waldorf. That was very good, because we spent time together and we all were going through the similar transition into this big public high school, trying to figure out what this was all about.

One of my biggest fears was that I wouldn't be up to speed with other students academically. And that fear was completely unfounded. Sophomore year I got into the drama program. In Waldorf school you do a class play every single year. My last year at Waldorf school my teacher brought in professional drama teacher, who worked with him on our play. She really trained us, and that was very exciting. That was when I started to love acting. I remember that particular year. I'd done it seven years before then, one through seven, and it hadn't really clicked with me, Eighth grade, they brought in this really good teacher, and it was great. That I carried on to Roosevelt, and it certainly prepared me better than most students.

Waldorf is about the arts, but not just the arts. It's about creativity, which is much more broadly based. You can do so much with being creative, learning to be creative. I believe creativity is something you can learn. I remember being in Waldorf, and no one ever talked about talent. We all were creative and artistic, everyone. But when you get to public school, people are always talking about talent, which I found difficult to stomach. It sets people apart. Here are the talented ones, here are the not-talented ones, the haves, the have-nots. That bothered me, even though I was considered to be in the talented group. It was very limiting for people to have that kind of discourse around them.

If every child is the union of body and soul, then every child deserves an opportunity for expression of his soul. For children, most of this potential for soul expression comes through aesthetics, through the arts. Ben's experience in the Waldorf school educated him about this insight and sensitized him to the disservice we do to children when we exclude them from a rich palette of artistic expressions, however "good" or "bad" they are at any particular form. In the Waldorf school, everyone draws, paints, sculpts, sings, plays musical instruments, dances, and acts.

Ben: Of course, people do have differences and even talents. But in the educational system, I much prefer it when students are spoken about in a way that's more about liberation and less about categorization.

A profound distinction.

Ben: At Waldorf school, even if I had not become so involved with drama, I still would have had that experience. Sometimes it's good to be involved with something creative even if you're not particularly good at it. At Waldorf the point of drama wasn't to make a very good play. The point was to get kids creating and involved and interacting, and everyone in the class doing it. And that's all good.

I really can't tell how much Waldorf affected me versus my parents' impacts. There's so much that goes into this. In high school I was definitely attracted towards groups and individuals who were creatively involved and had that kind of excitement about them. I think that kind of creativity and excitement happened to be strongest in the drama department and in the music department, both of which I got involved with. Both had strong student communities and teacher communities. In music I did vocal jazz. I only did it for a short time, but it introduced me to jazz music, which since then has become really important for me.

When I graduated from high school, I wanted to go to Williams College in Massachusetts. But they didn't want me. I got into Oberlin and Macalester, but they didn't offer enough scholarship. So I went to the University of Washington. My dad said, "The UW is a very good value if you look at it in terms of what you're getting for what you're spending." I have to say he was right, since I just paid off the last of my tuition debt. I've been working to do that, and now I'm really freed up to do what I want at this point.

Academically it was excellent. Socially, it was difficult. It's a very big school. I majored in international studies. I went to Vietnam the summer after my senior year in high school. It was my first time out of the country, and it was a wonderfully jarring experience. We raised money here in the states, which was used to pay for the de-mining of areas in the province that used to be the DMZ (demilitarized zone), the zone between north and south

Vietnam. We didn't speak any Vietnamese, and the students we met with didn't speak very much English. We painted the inside and outside of a kindergarten, and we did various community service activities in the area. So this trip got me interested in international studies.

When I graduated from college, I went to work for Elderwise, which is a senior enrichment program. I was actually working there before I graduated. I did ceramic art instruction with senior citizens. It was an art-and-physical-therapy program. I really enjoyed that and made some great friends through that community.

At the same time I was working in a summer program in West Seattle for students from Honduras. Unfortunately the money for that was cut, like so many other things. Then I worked awhile for Move On PAC. When that ended, I started working for a catering company. Also I'm volunteering for Seattle Arts and Lectures, doing grant prospect research for them.

So I'm still figuring out my plan. I really like educational settings, but I feel like I've spent so much time in academia and I've been so intellectually involved that I don't want to simply jump back into grad school. So I'm trying to figure out what's outside of that for now.

I'm not comfortable with letting things emerge so much as I really feel like I need to pursue them. I don't believe that things come to people. When I graduated last June from UW, I said I'd give myself a year to figure it out. So I'm still working on it.

Ben is centered in post-modern consciousness, as evidenced by the concerns he expresses and the work, however short-term, he has chosen so far. He also clearly feels empowered to make conscious decisions about where his life will go next.

Ben: Ecological problems and climate change are very much on my mind. I spent four and a half years in a university thinking about, writing about, talking about the large-scale problems. I've valued doing that. But I also felt at times that we were jumping over a certain gap in terms of scale, going from yourself and community out into the international arena. Now I feel that I need to pull in, to focus my energies locally—not only personally but also on what's around me. So I've also been working with statewide Poverty Action, doing citizen lobbying in Olympia for them, which is great.

I think the only downside to international studies is that it can be overwhelming if you try to look at it all at once, overwhelming and disempowering, because it's so huge. It makes you feel very small at times. So working locally has been more empowering, which is good. When I look at what's wrong around me, I feel that I have to do something. If I don't try, if I'm not somehow engaged and working on making things better, such as poverty or ecological problems, it's too depressing. I want to feel that I'm having an effect on things.

Responsibility, focus, conscience, and empowerment.

9   *LEE BENNER AND RICHARD KENAGY AND SARAH BENNER KENAGY*

Lee, Richard, and Sarah live in Seattle.

Lee: I was raised Catholic, and I started knowing more about esoteric Christianity in college. So my roots are Christian. As far as my parenting goes, it's my essential belief that I am more than just this body. There's a soul or a spirit here who's here for a purpose, and I need others to help keep that alive and draw that out. It is a process of waking up to my awareness of this, and then the unfolding is more finding a way to manifest that. I was remembering James Hillman, the book *The Soul's Code.* He used the image of the acorn—the acorn grows into the oak. Richard and I are going on 23 years of marriage and he is not the same man I said "I do" with. Life is a whole process. So that makes sense to me if I look at a child that way, too. I essentially feel that the children are a gift, and I know that parenting has grown me incredibly. So I just hold that there's something beyond, or something within each of them. My children are growing me as I'm growing them.

Lee articulates the profound insight: conscious parenting is an emotional, intellectual, and spiritual path in itself.

Lee: I was 28 when Sarah, our oldest, was born. We didn't start thinking about school until I was going back to work and looking at preschools. Some friends of ours were going to an open house at the Waldorf school, and it just sort of evolved from there. The longer we were in the school, the more we read, and the more it appealed to us. The school was in this old house then. On the outside it looked like the whole thing could fall apart. But when you walked inside, what I remember is this environment that was so soft and calm. Sarah previously had been at your kind of standard, run-of-the-mill day care, and there was just a different energy there. At Waldorf the whole form of play, the focus on rhythm -- I was learning about parenting, just that whole concept of having a rhythm in a child's life.

Young children in the first era of life particularly benefit from the experience of a daily rhythm consciously designed by parents, with a focus on balance between energetic and calm periods.

Richard: I grew up in such a way that essentially there was no spiritual life. There was some church, but I didn't have to do it, so it meant nothing. In college I was drawn to Eastern thinking. Even before that, I started karate. I didn't know anything other than I was drawn to it. I was drawn to Jung's writings. I didn't understand them; I was drawn to them. I'd been following my dreams since college, and you need someone to help you think about that. I went to John Hoff to help with dream interpretation. He got me into working my family of origin stuff. That's maybe a year before Sarah was born, so I'm about 28. But, again, spirituality really had no real meaning to me. I'm 46 now. This has been a period of learning about what spirit means to me, awakening to something that is a felt experience of spirit. Lee talked about how there has been a whole developmental sequence with us, and that has changed my parenting as a result. How we're raising Christopher, our youngest, is much different than how we raised Sarah, our oldest.

I think a big impact here is that in the road to awakening the spirit, there's been a whole period of working with my psychology: my ability to be a more pleasant person and lots of different things about my parenting style. There's big impact there. And my ability to feel and have a felt sense of Sarah's, Kaitlin's and Christopher's selves, their spirits. That's grown dramatically over the years, my sensitivity towards them.

Richard describes a quality of attention that guides him in perceiving his children as whole persons.

Richard: What happens for me has to do with just looking into the eyes of my children and having an intuitive sense that they will be awakened more than I am, and what's that going to be like? And so there's this sense of *they're in there,* but yet they're here like this right now. So there's continuity, that story that's going to happen there. It's more of a feeling than so many words.

Richard notes a common awareness that conscious parents have: that consciousness is evolving through them into their children's potentials and eventual manifestation as adults. He also acknowledges the intuitive capacity of a parent to feel his/her child's potential unfoldment.

Richard: Now that Sarah has grown up so much, she is affecting how I am as a parent with her and particularly with the other two kids. One conversation I can recall recently: Sarah was telling me that the way I was with her, it was hard on her. And I could do it differently and make it easier for both of us. She's right. At the same time the past is not something that I feel bad about. It's deeply affirming that Sarah can talk with us now in the way that she is able to. Poetry is something that I've begun enjoying lately in my life. So there are ways in which spirit is manifesting itself in my life that I think are impacting the kids. Yet it's not something that I directly say, this is spiritual.

Lee: Another part of our parenting—and it comes out of me— is carrying the roots of prayer life. I'm the one who, given our schedules, does the tuck-in. And with Sarah we prayed or we sang songs, or read by a candle, and she was baptized in the Catholic Church. I was actively going then, but I stopped, probably a little before Kaitlin was born. Then we had Kaitlin baptized just because I hadn't figured out anything else. Then when Christopher came along, but I hadn't found another church or parish that felt right for me, we had a christening. But throughout there was always a prayer in the evening. We always do blessing, now the Waldorf blessing. And the holidays for us have a seasonal focus and the Christian focus.

Lee's experience with prayer underlines the importance of ritual for children. The content of the prayer may change over time, but the felt sense of connection to something larger, deeper, is constant.

Lee: The other night we didn't do our prayer, and the kids just spontaneously started doing it. So at some level, children are spiritual. I'm going up to St. Pat's now. It was actually triggered by a conversation with Sarah, who at some point last year said, "You didn't raise me with any religion."

And I said, "That's true in the sense of like a church that we belong to, but do you feel you have a sense of what religion is?" She's a sensitive soul, she has a deep connection.

She said, "I don't know what I believe and I think there's a God, but—" I was sort of blown away because I had realized that I had depended on the Waldorf school curricula to keep that sense of spirituality alive. I realized that I might not have given Sarah enough of a base. The church is just a foundation, a grounding. And that's what I'm trying to put in place now for Kaitlin and Chris.

Kaitlin said, "If I'm older and if I don't want to keep going to a Catholic church will you be mad?"

I said, "No. I'm just giving you a base to push against, to explore from."

Lee echoes Inayat Khan's advice about the experience of conventional religion for children. Khan explains that engagement in the life of conventional religion is grounding for the child, even if the child chooses another spiritual path later in life.

Richard: The reason that I've kept our kids in the Waldorf school is my desire to keep their spark alive. I've seen that that has been true, and so we keep doing it. If I hadn't seen that, I would have not kept doing it. I turned off when I was a kid. I just left. There was a way I wouldn't share with the world who I really was. What I hope is that our kids stay open as long as they can, have the support and resources to cope or work with the bumps that happen, and still choose to stay at it, stay open. I see Sarah at almost eighteen as having that spark.

Lee: The curriculum in the Waldorf school keeps the arts not only alive but at the center of everything. I think that is really key. Perhaps I zero in on that because I didn't have that in my own childhood. Art was only on rainy Fridays, and the teacher said nice, and if you weren't an outstanding drawer that was it. The way that Waldorf relies on art as a form of expression is essential. What I've seen in terms of watching it over the years is it really allows the child's individuality to flourish. And they don't do grades, either, so instead of this comparison based on a label, who the children are can just flow. Everybody is different. And I think this experience gives kids that ground as an adult not to go out and compare, and then put a judgment on it, that somebody's better than the other or less than.

Richard: To grow into things naturally, rather than doing something by rote. Trusting that the child will grow into herself.

Richard states a central premise of the common vision: that we each embody a potential that is our own, that we can embody this potential, that parents need to trust the unfoldment of their child.

Lee: That trusting—with beginning to read as one example—that was a challenge with Sarah. She started reading in fourth grade, which is pretty late.

Very late, by modernist consciousness norms that say there is something wrong with a child who is not reading by age six.

Richard: But once she started, she liked to read, and she read, and it's never been a problem. It's never been an issue, and that's true for Christopher. He's seven now. And he'll read when he wants to read, although it will probably be earlier than his sisters just because he has two older sisters.

Lee's and Richard's trust in unfoldment has been validated by their experience with both of their two daughters.

Lee: With Sarah, when we were new at this, we read to her a lot, and we took trips to the library and everything. She just loved to be read to. I remember the summer before fourth grade and she still wasn't reading to herself. My parents were visiting, and they asked, "Are you sure?" I remember thinking, is this really going to happen? I was talking to one parent who had an older child and she said, "It will happen." And it did seem like just overnight; she got up one day and she was sitting and reading to herself.

Unless there is some organic brain dysfunction, children who live in a family culture of reading—where their parents read themselves and read to the child from infancy, where reading is valued and enjoyed—learn to read. There's a wide age range for the start date— from 3 years to 11 or 1or even later—but once the reading begins, children quickly become capable readers and usually can read anything within a few years. The idea that reading skill develops one year at a time is falsehood generated by the grade level structure of modernist schooling.

Richard: Kaitlin has gone to the University of Washington summer camp for three years, and she was running into some peer judgment of not being able to read. That was somewhat hard for her. But last year, third grade, she started to read.

Lee: At the summer camp the way I just told them, "Yes, she's in second grade. Yes, she's in third grade, and she doesn't read or write now." So for language arts they would have her do the picture and tell the story, and one of the teachers would write down the story for her. They didn't make a big deal of it, which I really appreciated. And I said to her, "If kids are giving you a hard time you can say, 'Well, that's true that I don't read yet, but I do speak

Japanese and Spanish, and I do play the flute.'" I said, "Your curriculum is different; it says nothing about you as a person." It took awhile, but I believe this has strengthened her feeling that "I can be different and that's okay."

There was another time, I remember, just before Kaitlin was going into first grade. We were looking at the cost of the Waldorf school for two kids. I went to an open house at our local alternative public school. I remember going into their kindergarten, and there were the letters just like I had as a kid, and the chalk, the list of words, cat and dog. Just the feel of it was that it was only an intellectual schoolhouse, and that's all there is and that's what they throw at the kids. I just thought, no, I can't go that route.

Now we have a 17-year old listening to the new wave rock station. You know, "I'm a rat in a cage." And Christopher was 5, going, "I'm just a rat in a cage." We realize that second and third children are just exposed naturally to more media. It's not fair for us to say to Sarah, "You can never listen to your music in the car."

Kaitlin turned 12 in December. There are 11 girls in Kaitlin's class. Kaitlin is really into soccer, and she loves to read. Some of the other girls are listening more to the rock stations. Kaitlin still likes the baggy clothes, and she doesn't like to talk about boys. Some of the girls are all into boys, and some, like Kaitlin, aren't. We talk about this some, and she'll say, "They just talk about things that I'm not interested in." When Sarah's around, she says, "That's okay, Kaitlin, you do what you want to do, it'll be alright." So she's getting those messages, but there's still some wrestling, some tension.

When children enter the second era of childhood and engage with the world beyond the family, parents both need to continue to express their own values and give the child enough space to explore her/his own knowing. Life is about experience—and what one makes of this experience.

Richard: We try to protect our kids from a lot of what's out there in the media. So much of it is not good. In the neighborhood even kids in the early elementary grades see all kinds of movies. We tend to be very limited on television exposure, although they do see plenty of TV. And I don't know what all, they can definitely sneak TV in other places and we wouldn't necessarily know. Same with computer games that may be around. So it's not like I'm expecting them not to be exposed to it. It's going to happen, but we do want to moderate it.

Lee: The TV used to be not turned on without a special purpose in our house. But what has changed is we have a 17-year old who watches TV. So we have to deal with the "how come Sarah's watching and we don't get to watch TV" from the other kids.

Richard: She gets to watch lots more than the other two do.

Lee: When Christopher gets upset at school, one thing his teacher has him do is put his head down on his desk and listen for the quiet voice inside. And she asked what I thought about that, and I said, "Well, right on." At such an early age, helping them identify that they can go inside. When I talk to him about his anger, he's real clear. He says, "I get hot all over, I get hot inside, and I see red." You couldn't have a clearer picture than that. It still comes out very explosive. The key is letting him have that without any shame, without saying it's wrong, acknowledging it, that's a feeling just like other feelings and they need to express themselves.

****

This interview took place two years later.

Lee: During the past two years we have worked to be more consistent in parenting. Because now that Sarah's grown, we can see that the things we did teach her are some of what she's been able to work on as a young adult. When she finished high school, she had a number of dreams and couldn't find it in herself to really act on any of them. It took her six months or so to decide what she wanted to do. She was just working. But once she decided on a direction, it's been impressive to watch her stay with it, to get up at

5:30 in the morning and go at it. I've been quite proud of her, and it's a delight to see her have her creativity and do what she wants to do.

Now as a young adult she needs to work with the money management. She and I have an agreement that before she moves out of the house next spring, we'll sit down and work this out. She doesn't have a checkbook anymore; she just uses a debit card and doesn't tally things. I kid her, because my dad was a banker, that he's up in heaven just pulling his hair out at the way she's taking care of her money.

We are changing our relationship with her. She is a young adult. That was a conscious choice. When she graduated from high school, she was 18. We've had a shift in how we act. She still lives at home, but it's on a different basis than before. And it's worked for everyone.

Lee continues to be coherent with the common vision's principle of providing freedom with safe boundaries. She acknowledges the new stage in Sarah's unfoldment with awareness and respect, yet she still engages in protecting Sarah in an appropriate way, as shown in his discussion about money.

Lee: We're very open with our children about the work we're doing to wake up, to grow ourselves. And it's been good to share that with Sarah in particular. She was clearly stuck in her life because of her own anxiety, which I got it from my mother and passed on to her. I'm working to change it and I told her, "You can change." And that shift has been happening. So it's been a gift that she's still here right now while we've been doing this work for our own growth. And, of course, there are still challenges. She's not always consistent in doing what she should around the house.

Richard: It's that thing about wanting to contribute to the whole. She wants to, but it's the follow-through that is inconsistent. She'll do some stuff that's just out of her own energy and good will, and then there are other things where she'd not get it done.

Inevitably most late adolescents/young adults are going to be inconsistent. This is another time of transition, and every transition in unfoldment from one stage to another evokes inconsistency. Two steps upwards, one step back.

Richard: Sarah does have a lot of freedom. But our family life has also changed. In many ways she precipitated our looking at ourselves and our family. Lee and I are working on these underlying unconscious issues and are changing, and I think this change has allowed Sarah not to need to go away just yet.

Another insight from the common vision that Lee and Richard live is the invitation to experience conscious parenting as a vehicle for their own psychological and spiritual growth.

Lee: Kaitlin will be 15 next week. She's very different from Sarah, and we're different. We're more relaxed and more able to talk things through. She's a freshman in our local public high school. She went through eight years at the Waldorf school. Last year she spent a lot of time in her room reading. She's very artistic, so she had that and soccer and school and one close friend, and so that was pretty well her world.

She was very clear about what she wanted—to go to the public high school. And now she's just blossomed. It's been incredible to see. She's vivacious now, our introvert. She'll sit and talk about what she's learned and what she's doing and who did this in class and who got her in trouble and made her laugh. So she's really hit her stride right now. She was happy at the Waldorf school mostly, but she was ready to go on.

Richard: She misses some of the people from Waldorf, the relationships there and the bonding of her class. But even before this year she was into the wider world of fantasy through her reading.

Lee: All through Waldorf school, even in eighth grade, Kaitlin's main attire was soccer shorts and large t-shirts. The parents of other Waldorf girls would make comments to me last year about this. "There's Kaitlin, she's in that soccer stuff." She'd show up at a dance, and that was her choice. I was fine with that. By eighth grade the other girls in her class were wearing whatever they could get away, given the Waldorf dress code, and some of them really pushed it to the limits. It was the moms of those girls who made comments to me about Kaitlin's choice of attire. And I thought, it's fine; she has such a strong sense of self that she's going to dress the way she wants.

Lee supports Kaitlin's expression of her own identity, her own authenticity at that stage of her unfoldment.

Lee: This October she asked if she could go shopping for clothes. We never had before. She had t-shirts from fourth grade and Sarah's old stuff. I said fine, and now she's dressing more consciously. It's just blue jeans and t-shirts that fit rather than loose ones, and she still doesn't want to do makeup or anything else. So it's a shift. Now she's stepped into that world, but she still has her own sense of how she wants to meet it.

Kaitlin sounds very much like an adolescent who has been invited to discover herself. Thus she knows how to maintain her integrity while she accommodates as much as needed to establish her membership in her new social milieu.

Lee: Chris is in fourth grade now. He's in the Waldorf school. His reading is really coming along this year.

Richard: He's put some work into that, and writing seems to one of the things that really caught him. He had to write stories, and he is really getting into that.

Lee: He's learning to express himself well. The teacher's really helped him with that. He's able to put into words what's going on with him. It's a challenge in terms of having a 15-year old and a 20-year old in the house and still trying to keep some kind of a boundaries for a 10-year old. He's only 10. Even with the music that's chosen when we're in the car. Last year Kaitlin would always test us and put on the alternative rock station and I'd say, "No." It took months before she finally stopped just trying to listen to that station when Chris was in the car. There's a real mix in his class. Some parents have a lot of videos and movies and TV. You definitely see the impact of it.

Richard: Even at the Waldorf school, people are mixed about the effects of TV. But there are studies, and then analyses of multiple studies. That violence on TV does have an effect on children.

Lee: I was just talking about that with another Waldorf parent. She has two sons in the kindergarten, and she's finding herself shocked that other parents are letting their kindergartners watch TV. She said, "I chose this because I wanted to be surrounded by people who were doing what I am, which is no TV at all now." She wants the teachers to tell the parents, no TV. But I don't see the teachers being able to do that. They tell parents about the negative effects, but then parents do what they will.

Richard: To have a good family, you've got to have good relationships. To have good relationships, you have to work on yourself, consciously.

Lee: It's all about how you view your child. It takes being aware that there's a person there. There's a person in a little body, and they need to be treated with respect and called out, not pushed out.

Richard and Lee summarize two key values of the common vision.

****

Sarah Benner Kenagy at 18

One thing that I've recently realized that has been really helpful was the kind of sheltered atmosphere that I grew up in. Now I see young girls who are constantly exposed and bombarded by the media, and I don't feel that I was really exposed to that until later. It was starting in sixth grade that the media really started to affect me. I think that that was really helpful, because when I was exposed to the media I was a lot more able to discern—it's just an image, not reality.

Sarah explains why the ways that her parents protected her as a young child allowed her to bring a critical awareness to mass culture when she did begin to access it.

Sarah: When I was not allowed to see TV and movies, I remember being really upset at times. I wanted to be able to watch. I had friends who were in public school, and even then I could see the huge difference between their education and my education. Even so, starting in fourth grade, I think, but definitely in fifth grade, I was frustrated by the limitations. It escalated up through the years until eighth grade we were just so ready to get out of Waldorf school. Looking back now I think it was definitely a good thing for me to be there. And kids always want what they can't have or what their other friends are having.

I feel like the Waldorf education I got was much more nurturing. The teachers really got to know each student. It wasn't preaching to the class. They really were with us. It's supposed to be all eight years, but in my case we had one teacher for first grade and then another teacher for second and third, and then a teacher from fourth through eighth.

It really became like a second family that was comfortable to grow up in. And also not getting letter grades I think really helped. In high school letter grades are just so important, and no matter what you do to get that, it doesn't matter. Just get that A. And with Waldorf it was more, you can improve on this, so let's see how you can improve on this. It was a lot more geared towards improving and learning more rather than let's get this A.

Steiner's Waldorf School is a brilliant integral educational model. The qualities that Sarah notes as nurturing for her can be—and are—embodied in a variety of holistic educational forms.

Sarah: Another thing at Waldorf is what they do with reading. I know that I learned to read a lot later than kids in the public schools. I think in the public schools you first start to learn the letters in kindergarten. In my memory I didn't start to really learn how to read until I want to say third grade. I think that I was a little slower than most kids, but the thing about reading in Waldorf is that they don't shove it on the student. I think because they didn't do that, now I love to read; I just gobble up books. And the friends that I had who were in public schools, they hated books; you couldn't get them to read one. So I think that because it wasn't forced on me and shoved down my throat, I'm a lot more able to enjoy reading.

A key principle of the common vision: invite the child to set the course of her own learning, according to her unfolding interest, curiosity, and passion. Trust the unfoldment of capability and talent.

Sarah: I remember being a little embarrassed when my friends would ask me about why I couldn't read yet. There was this one experience that I had, I just remembered it. I went to Sunday School once, and this must have been in first grade. The rules were going around, and everyone was asked to read them. I didn't know how to read, and everyone else who was my age could read. That was just so embarrassing. Looking back now I have no hard feelings about that, not at all.

After 8th grade I left Waldorf and went to public high school. I wanted to go, but it was really hard at first. My graduating class from eighth grade was only eight people, including me. Then to go to a public school where my freshman class was close to 400 people. I would talk to my mom about this, and I would cry about having to go there sometimes because it was just so different. I remember being really shy. I had friends, but it was like I really tried to get that small environment that I had at Waldorf. It was a lot easier transition for some of my other friends, but for me it was really difficult. Also the whole getting up and changing classrooms instead of having the teachers come in was strange.

I think the biggest shock was the relationship between student and teacher in public school—it's so different. Waldorf is really geared toward work with the individual and how we can help you to learn.

In public school, because all the teachers have so many students, they can't give that individual time. So it's much less personal. That was hard. It still bothers me. You don't have the convenience of having someone there who, if you have just a simple little question, can answer it for you. You have to ask someone else or stay after school, if the teacher has the time to do that. It's just so different, and that really shocked me.

By sophomore year I was used to the whole routine, but I didn't really start to enjoy going there and being comfortable in it until halfway through sophomore year. I did love it after that, just the social aspect of it. But it took a long time for me to get used to it.

Sarah comes to love her large public high school because of the "social aspect," her peer group and friends, not the academics.

Sarah: As for grades and tests, it was something to get used to. At first it was neat getting letter grades and having the tests and all that, because we didn't have that at Waldorf. But especially this past year, my senior year, it's like I've just begun to realize that I can't stand having the tests and the grades because that's all you're viewed on, your grades, and there's so much more to a person. I am not a very good test taker when it comes to math and science. I can understand something, but the way that it's presented to me on the test, or having it all drop down to this number, is really hard. Still that really bothers me, and I know it bothers a lot of my friends, too. You're viewed as this number. And there's so much more to you, but it's all in this little number.

Sarah's critique of the depersonalized quality of modernist schooling is informed by the contrast between this model and her Waldorf school experience.

Sarah: In high school I found that I was much more mature than a lot of my friends. I hate the way that sounds, but I'm not bragging—It's just the way it is. I've never really been bothered by what people thought of me. You see these images of high schools girls. They are in these little cliques. They are into what are we

149

going to wear today and what's the dance. There are girls like that in my class, but that never really interested me. I always played the role of mediator between my friends, where I would help them step back and really view the situation instead of just being mad and lashing out. I think that for where I am right now, I'm a lot more developed as a human, if that makes sense, than where my friends are. And I think, I know that Waldorf had a huge part in that, because they're so focused on developing a person as well as teaching us.

While Sarah's maturation was certainly promoted by her Waldorf experience, as she notes, her parents' respect for her personhood most certainly also played a role in her unfoldment.

Sarah: I'm able to step back and look at things. I mean, not always. I was talking with my friend from Waldorf days, and we're actually really close now, still. She basically said the same things that I've been saying. It's bothered her, the difference between the level of maturity she's at and the level her friends are at, because they are so caught up in themselves and they can't see the bigger picture. I'm in touch with three of the people I graduated with from Waldorf, and we all have this same sense of things.

Since all of these parents chose the Waldorf school experience for their children, it's reasonable to assume that they shared its values and acted from them, more or less, at home.

Sarah: I know that my Waldorf friends are all very thankful for going to Waldorf, and I know that there also has been a process for us to realize that. There was bitterness all through eighth grade. We were 13 through 14, and just ready to go out and we didn't want to be protected anymore. It was really frustrating, because we had all these rules that seemed so insignificant. Now looking back we know that maybe they were insignificant, but they were helpful, even if we didn't know it then.

When Steiner created the first Waldorf school in 1919, Germans youths ages 13-14 were children. There were no adolescents, as we understand this stage of unfoldment today. Now these 13 year olds— and sometimes even 11 year olds—are adolescents. Since the Waldorf school teacher achieves a quasi-parental role over eight years with the same class, naturally and inevitably the teens begin to distance themselves from their Waldorf teacher in 6th, 7th, and 8th grade just as they push away from their parents. Unfortunately the Waldorf school model has not yet evolved to respond to these evolutionary changes in the timetable and stages of human unfoldment.

Sarah: I'm not planning on going directly to college. I actually just got a part-time job, and I'm looking for a second part-time job so I can save money to travel. It's not the type of travel where I'm going to be staying in four-star hotels. I really want to travel and live in a place and get to know it. I guess I just want to see what else is out there before I try to figure out what I want to do with the rest of my life.

What started me on this whole thing was my junior year when I spent two months in Japan as an exchange student, and it just blew me away. My whole life I lived in Seattle, and this is all I had been exposed to. Then being exposed to this entirely different culture—I can't imagine right now, in my life, not exploring what else is out there.

My parents have been really supportive. When I first said, "I don't want to go to college next year," it was never an argument because they really don't want me to do something that I don't want to do if it's not going to benefit me. If I don't think it's going to benefit me, why make me do it? So they've been nothing but supportive and trying to help me figure out how I'm going to do it. It's very helpful to know that my parents are not saying, "Oh, you can't do that, you're not ready for that, you're only 18, how do you think you can go around the world?" It's never been like that. I strongly believe that this is where I'm at right now, this is what will be helpful. And because I feel so strongly about that, they really have accepted it. I'm sure they're a little worried, but it hasn't been anything that they've been trying to persuade me to do something else.

Lee's and Richard's respect for and trust in Sarah is evident in her perception of her parents.

Sarah: I'm hoping that this traveling will focus me a little more, or that I'll discover something that I want to do for the rest of my life. I know that I want to work with children. And I think just being exposed to different cultures will help me. So it's not so much that I'm going to find my calling, but I think that this will definitely help me to see that there are other things out there.

It really bothers me how many people in my age group, just either don't care, or don't care to know what is happening outside their own little world. They're thinking if they don't know, it will take care of itself or it doesn't affect them. But it bothers me that so many people are just willing to accept what's presented to them without question, be okay with that and settle for that and live their own little life. I think that so many people are just jaded, because so many people in the world don't have the luxury to worry about anything but themselves, and we do. We live in these big houses, have so much opportunity to do different things, and yet there are so many people who are wasting that and not caring, not willing to do something, not willing to step outside their comfort zone, to open up their eyes to see what else is there, if they can possibly help.

My goal has never been to just make money. I need to make money—money is necessary, but that's never been my goal. I want to make a difference, and I know that's kind of a cliche, but I don't want to feel like I haven't done anything to help anybody else beside myself.

Sarah is clearly centered in post-modern consciousness at the age of 18, as evidenced in these comments.

Sarah: I think every generation does multiple things wrong. It's this cycle. Every generation before the one that is young now, or my generation, this is the same for my parents' generation. Of course there are some things that anger you that you wish they would have done differently, but every generation has to compensate for what the one before has left them.

Sarah expresses an insight about the human condition and a compassion for her elders that far transcends her chronological age

Sarah: I was baptized Catholic, but I've never regularly gone to church. And although I do have this sense of there being something greater than just the physical, I don't know what it is. I don't believe that God is a he, and it's this person who, not person, but this God who says, this is a sin and you can't do that and if you do that, then too bad, you can't come up to heaven, you're going to hell. I don't know if I believe in hell. I don't think I do. I do believe in reincarnation. So I do have a sense of the spiritual, but it's not anything that could be summed up into one religion.

I have friends who deeply believe in the Christian religion, where what happens is God's will and if I'm having a problem I can pray. And they believe that an answer will come to them. I don't have that, and I think that in ways that would be a lot easier. At the same time, I think that they didn't have a chance to ask themselves if that's really what is right for them, because it was chosen by their parents and put on them. And I have—it's not so clear but there's something greater than me, and it doesn't have those kind of boundaries.

****

This interview was two years later.

Sarah: I'm 20 now. I changed direction since we talked before. I'm going to South Seattle Community College, in their baking and pastry program, for over a year now.

I had been working full time for about a year. My idea was that I was going to save up enough money and just go off, start travelling. But that didn't happen, and I found myself really unsatisfied and didn't know what I was going to do. I was just kind of stuck, and I didn't know what was going to happen next. I'd been feeling this way for a couple months, and my mom said one day, "I know you like to bake, I know you've always liked to do this and South Seattle Community College has one of the best programs in the country right now." So I looked into it and signed up and started going, and this was all within a week that the next quarter started. I just started right in there. And it turned out to be a really good thing. I'm really enjoying it.

I knew that I didn't want to go right to college. I didn't feel like I'd be able to plop myself down and be studious and really use the money that was going into it well. It didn't feel right to me. Now I'm working toward an associates degree as I do the baking program. Maybe I'll try to get a job at a small bakery for awhile, or try large-scale, like grocery store. But I really do enjoy it, so I think I'll be doing this for a while now.

The conventional next step for Sarah would have been an undergraduate college career, but her self-knowledge—and the trust she had in this knowing, despite some difficulties and challenges—led her to make a different choice.

Sarah: I think my parents are really happy that I'm actually following through with something, and of course that I'm enjoying it. They're both really happy that I am working towards a degree at the same time. They've both been really, really supportive of just whatever choice I wanted to make, and they were pretty careful about not forcing anything on me but more helping me in a certain way, if that was what I wanted to do. When I was in that unhappy period, they saw that I was really dissatisfied with what I was doing, and they got me talking about what I thought I could be doing right now that would be better? So they were really helpful in that way.

Lee and Richard maintained their nurturing stance toward Sarah in a way that both supported her and respected her dignity.

Sarah: I find that I move really easily between all the different age groups. When I first started at South Seattle, I was the youngest in my program by about eight years, so I became friends with a lot of older people than I am. It was comfortable for me. I'm not sure how it was for them. I'm sure I was regarded at first as this little 19-year old, what does she know? But we all get along really well. It's a really diverse age group, from the sixties all the way down to me and now someone who is 18 years old. I'm not even really aware of age anymore, if I ever was. I just get to know the person.

I feel lucky that my parents protected me from some things when I was young. I think I have a stronger sense of who I am from that somehow; it has a lot to do with the fact that I wasn't overly exposed to certain things. And I definitely still feel a little farther along on the emotional maturity ladder than some other people my age, or even older than me, as I'm dealing with them now.

I still don't attend any church. But recently I have started reading some spiritual poetry. So it's something that I think about, but the thought of organized religion doesn't attract me. So spirituality is something that I'm learning about on my own.

I'm not really sure how I want to talk about spirituality. It is something that is there for me. I have a sense that it is part of me I just don't have it structured in the sense that I have names for certain aspects of it.

When I look out at the larger world, I look at it with some confusion at this point. I get really frustrated when I talk to people my own age about world events because for the most part they don't know about them. Something that I attribute to my Waldorf education is the fact that I do pay attention to what's going on in the world, and I don't so much cut it off from where I am, living here in Seattle, in the United States. It's frustrating to me when I look around and my general sense is that people my own age or even older than me just don't seem to have an open mind or don't seem to care about the bigger scale. I have a hard time understanding why people ignore what's going on.

I guess they are just in their own little worlds. I guess I just have a better sense of what's going on somewhere else, so I'm not necessarily stuck in this one place. I don't mean to sound cheesy in any way, but I feel more that the world is more connected or just smaller, in a sense, than I think a lot of people think. And that's what frustrates me. When I hear people just shrug off or disregard issues that are a big deal in other countries, it's like, oh, if we don't think about it, it will go away, or what could we do about it? I don't always know what we could do about it, but the fact that you're not even acknowledging it isn't going to help anything. I believe that Waldorf helped me learn to put more meaning into things than I think people get if they go to public schools.

Sarah's global-centric consciousness is another clear marker of post-modern consciousness.

Sarah: What I learned is that it's not just all about you. And when it is about you, it's also about what could you do to help the bigger picture.

At school I was in charge of five other students at a station where we were doing breads together. One was a 60-year old man. We got off to a rocky start and were having some problems. I felt that he was disregarding everything I was saying. And I was thinking it was because I'm 40 years younger than him and he felt, what does she know, I'm just going to do it my own way.

After the first week, I took him aside and raised the issues directly with him. We talked about all these different things, and it was a really good talk because afterwards when we had gotten the issues dealt with, we could then do our work well together.

I see other people my age—and older—who when they're having a problem with someone, instead of actually dealing with the person, they'll go talk about it with other people. And that usually doesn't help.

I just want to figure things out and make them work, and I can often do that. And I know that acting out from the emotions doesn't solve anything. I also know that your emotional maturity definitely has an impact on whether or not you're going to care about more than just yourself.

David Marshak

10 KEN AND ALISA MALLOCH AND JORDAN MALLOCH

Ken and Alisa live in Seattle. Jordan lives near Seattle.

Ken: The key values I brought to parenting were freedom and imagination. You encourage the child to imagine and then be sure the child has the freedom to go and work with that imagination.

Ken's values are in deep alignment with the common vision.

Alisa: The Waldorf School was really nice for us. It was like a co-parenting group. We didn't have family nearby for a good portion of our kids' lives, so it was good to have Waldorf School show us some of the values that were quite new. We hadn't really done a lot of pre-work, and so you stumble along sometimes. So the Waldorf school helped to bring out the importance of creativity.

Freedom and imagination and creativity.

Ken: We first learned about Waldorf from a Belgian family that we knew in Saudi Arabia. The images of Waldorf really captured our imagination as being significantly different. So when we came to Seattle, this image really attracted us. So we tracked down the Waldorf School here. Jordan went there for six years, through 8th grade. He went to Nathan Hale High School for two years and then into Running Start. He wasn't being really challenged in high school. And he also was getting very involved with paddling—competitive canoeing—at that point. Running Start was good for him. It gave him space to do what he wanted, and then it helped him move on faster towards college, which actually turned out to be really good.

Alisa: Jordan also had a lot of experience being away from home. He'd been away all summer and away because of sports. So he was ready to be out of high school and in the junior college.

Ken: I never cease to be amazed at the depth at which the experience of Waldorf school in Jordan's formative years keeps bubbling up and resurfacing. I think it gave him a greater depth and understanding than he would have achieved elsewhere. And I think that it stood him in good stead to be able to handle things that were beyond his years chronologically.

Alisa: The joke in the family is that when you have a kid in adolescence, you want them to find something they can be totally focused on to keep them on the straight and narrow. And the joke is that we got Jordan focused so much on canoeing that we can't get him unfocused.

Adolescence can often be a time for great concentration if the youth has the freedom to live his passion. This concentration challenges the youth to learn to operate his will in service of his goals.

Alisa: I think his sport helped him a great deal in that period. It gave him a lot of self-esteem. And he had a good balance with his education. He also had a part-time job during that time, and he was socially very active. So I think that it did take up a lot of his time. I think kids can do more than one thing. I think you need to challenge a child at that point.

Ken: It's a delicate balance. You don't really know until after the fact. Jordan was also fortunate in having a group of friends who were very fine people in their own right. They formed their own community of support. If he had not had that, he may not have been quite so successful.

Alisa: And Jordan is married now. He was married in September. They got married in Spain. Our daughter went to the Waldorf school through fifth grade. But then a lot of her friends left, and they didn't have a really strong teacher for that class. She wanted to go elsewhere, so we went with that.

Ken: I was even on the board of the Waldorf school at that point, but it was clear to us that this was not working for her. So we made the decision she'd no longer be a student there. There were some interesting discussions, but you've got to do the right thing.

The Mallochs' sensitivity to their children as unique and different individuals is evidenced by this decision.

Alisa: So she went to the alternative middle school, New Options (a progressive public middle school in Seattle founded by a group of parents) for a year. We looked at several middle schools, and she chose New Options. That was a good transition year for her, but then at the end of the year, she said, "If I have to talk about feelings or computers one more minute..." So she switched to traditional schools, Eckstein Middle School and Garfield High School. And she finished up at Garfield, all the way through. We didn't put pressure on her. When she wanted to do things, we let her do them. We encouraged our children to live their own ways.

The Mallochs' daughter's expression of her own freedom led her to conventional public secondary schools, and her parents respected her decisions.

Alisa: Our youngest went to a Waldorf preschool and a Waldorf kindergarten. Then he went all the way through the eighth grade at the Waldorf school itself. He went to Nathan Hale High School for two years—

Ken: But he didn't really enjoy it, so he transferred to Garfield High School. We were apprehensive about that, because Garfield is so much larger. But he was insistent, so we followed his lead.

Alisa: Garfield has a really good outdoor program. He really wanted to be part of that.

Ken: There's only one chance. It's not like you've got a spare child over here to practice on. Is it divinely driven? I don't know. But we wanted our kids to have the freedom, the inspiration, the vision for their own lives.

****

Jordan Malloch at 25:

I went to public school in Houston. When we moved to Seattle, my parents found the Waldorf school and I went there from third grade on. My class had the same teacher from second grade on, so I only knew one Waldorf teacher, Karen Burch. That was a great thing. In December we had a memorial for her. Unfortunately she passed away a year ago February, from cancer.

I remember a sense of definitely belonging to the class, because we were such a cohesive unit. We had the same teacher all the time. We didn't go from class to class with different kids; you had your grade and your class. I still remember the people in my class, even though some didn't stay the whole time. At one point in fifth grade I was the only boy in my class. It was a bunch of girls and myself.

We went on trips together. I remember that the first week I was in Waldorf school, we went on a trip to my teacher's house on Orcas Island. That was definitely a big moment. You meet this group of new people, and all of the sudden you're going on this trip with these people you've never met before.

I was coming from a public school background to this Waldorf school, so it was a pretty big eye opener. Learning new ways, learning different things. I just enjoyed it a lot. I remember a sense of enjoyment, that's one of the biggest memories I have.

Even though a lot of these kids had been together for a few years already, I fit in pretty well, pretty quickly. And they were very accepting, too. I'm usually pretty good at making friends. So socially it was pretty easy.

But the school part was very different. It never occurred to me that it was weird or anything like that. It just was what it was. I like to learn. So we're playing recorder today? Alright. We play flute today, we do eurythmy. Okay. I didn't like eurhythmy by the end, but looking back on it, it wasn't the worst thing in the world, either.

By sixth grade our class started to get a little more contentious because we were going through adolescence. More confrontation with the teacher, especially in the eighth grade year. I had a really good friend who decided not to go to Waldorf in eighth grade. So that was a little tough for me—my best friend left. But I still felt like I learned a lot, and I still enjoyed the education. I was ready to go to high school, though, there's no question about that.

Sixth and seventh grades were a lot of fun for me. Eighth grade I kind of moved on. It was a kind of a transition year for me, looking towards the next part of my life. Also I started canoeing, which took a lot of my time as well. My mom signed me up for a canoe class, and I really enjoyed it. I really got into the competitive part, so that made a big difference. It changed me a lot, and I resented that a little bit, because it made me different from most of the kids I knew. I was really focused. And I felt like I was better than they were. And they were hanging out and just not doing a whole lot, and every day I was out training. And that added to me not getting along with people that well in 8th grade. The class was like a family, and I had sort of left before we actually left.

Mostly though I really liked Waldorf. Karen definitely made learning very interesting. She could really teach history so well. I love history, and I attribute a lot of that to her. She also taught geography. I love to travel, and I think that connects to her, too, because she made the fables and historical stories come alive. She told very good stories.

We received such an all-encompassing education, from all around the globe, touching on Norse myths and Indian myths and Native

American, all over. And we learned that we're not just citizens of America, but that we are also citizens of the world. There is history beyond America and there are people around the world, and there are reasons that we're different and reasons that we're the same.

When I went to Hale High School, that was a pretty big transition. It was definitely a lot more restrictive. You had to do things a certain way, and I didn't have that freedom that you get with Waldorf. I didn't yearn to be back with my class, but at the same time it was definitely an awakening in a different sense.

I didn't take to it that well. That's why I did Running Start. After my sophomore year at Hale I started doing Running Start full-time at North Seattle Community College because I felt like I just wanted to get going with my education.

My mom always believed that I could be better than I thought I could be. She thought that I wasn't getting a whole lot out of high school. At that point Hale was fairly marginal. I was in honors classes, but she didn't think I was being challenged and she said, "You should do Running Start instead." So she was very supportive.

It also worked very well with paddling, because I had more breaks in the class schedule and I could go to races more. And classes started later so I could train in the morning, train in the afternoon. So it all came to a crux and it worked out very well for what I was doing at the time. I knew what I wanted to do, and my parents were very supportive of me doing it.

I've always related well to people who are older than me. I've always had friends who were older. Both in Running Start and in paddling competitions, most of the people were older than me. So that made Running Start easier.

In community college the expectation was that you get your work done. Most of the students were older, and everybody was pretty supportive, especially people who were there as serious students. They were trying to go on to a four-year university. They gave me a lot of appreciation for my contributions. We had a lot of study groups together, and I always did my share and sometimes more.

I did have some other friends at North Seattle who were doing Running Start, so they were my age. We were able to hang out, so we had some commonality. But I never felt I got treated poorly at North because I was younger.

When I finished Running Start, I was one quarter short of graduating with my A.A. So I finished my degree and then went to the University of Washington 's business school. I went there off and on for the last couple of years. It took me a while to graduate because I was training and racing. So I never went there more than two quarters consecutively.

Training takes a lot of time. And there are world championships in my event, the two-man canoe, every year. I started competing in those seven years ago, and I competed in the last two Olympics. This year the world championship is in Zagreb, Croatia. I plan to keep competing through the next Olympics, and then I'll still paddle and race locally—and paddle to keep in shape. I don't want to stop that part of my life. But I'm definitely going to focus more on my career at that point. I really want to have my own business. My dad's a big influence in my life, and he's an entrepreneur.

I expect it will involve international business. I was born in the U.S., but for the first five years of my life I didn't live a whole lot in the U.S. My parents moved to England and then we moved to Saudi Arabia, and then to Houston. It was my dad's job. He had an irrigation company. My dad is from Australia, and Mom's Canadian. I don't always get a chance to travel after races, but I do get a sense of the culture. I've been to a lot of places in Europe, northern Africa, and elsewhere.

I view myself as a citizen of the world as much as a citizen of the country. I am definitely an American, but that doesn't trump my world citizenship. And I think that world view does come from the education I received at a young age.

As for the future, I don't think we're in the best situation right now. But at the same time, I feel like we have a possibility to move forward, and that's something I feel personally involved in. We need to talk with people and understand their views. America is a great country, but there are other people outside our borders that we are affecting, whether we like it or not. It's not just us and only us.

For me, if I did have my own company and it was a successful company, I'd like to have it be a just company and an environmentally sound company, something that can influence and help to move things in a positive direction. This is definitely a driving factor in my life.

I do believe in capitalism. It's a good thing. But I think that directed capitalism can be even more effective. We need incentive capitalism that is effective for the right values. That can be very powerful.

Jordan's articulation of his values suggests that he is accessing integral consciousness. He wants to integrate the values of modernism—capitalism and nation state—with the values of post-modernism: planetary identity, respect for other cultures, environmental responsibility, and justice.

11 EVOLUTIONARY PARENTING

Beth Lye, a parent in Seattle, told me, "*I see children as travelers. Children are way more than just physical; there's the soul and spiritual element to them. I don't feel like I have too much say in where my children go. I feel like I'm here as a caretaker. I knew I would have a child, and I was pretty positive it was a girl, and I knew I would nurse her. And I didn't realize at first that her path would be a path of development for me. I didn't realize how much I was going to change in relation to her. And I think change for the better. I didn't realize that was going to happen, or that I would have to make really hard decisions, or think about things differently. I'm trying not to have expectations, because I feel like I want to leave her free, and approach my daughter with an open heart and with guidance. The idea of the 'inner teacher' does make sense to me. I feel that I've been guided in my life—that there are certain ways and paths that I chose to take, that I'm not always sure where my choices come from but they get me to the place I need to go. So, yes, I believe that my children are unfolding from someplace, and there must be their own pattern being revealed.*"

Beth describes the essentially paradoxical quality of evolutionary parenting with grace and self-knowledge. Our children are ours, and they are their own selves. *Evolutionary parenting is always holding, holding, holding—but with inevitably greater challenge, letting go, letting go. Letting go, within safe boundaries.* Each parent who speaks in this book has her or his own voice, yet they are speaking from a shared set of insights and understandings.

- Parenting with the guidance of the values described in the *common vision* is challenging, because it requires parents to navigate a consciously discovered path between their own values—attending to, honoring, and following the child's soulful expression—and the mainstream culture. Evolutionary parenting requires a profound commitment to one's values, openness to learning and one's own personal growth, and the courage and commitment to return to this path of parenting despite inevitable deflections and temporary failures.

- The first era of childhood requires a great deal of protection of the child's natural consciousness from the lures of the mainstream culture, and this must be done without hooking the child with the "forbidden fruit" narcotic.

- The second era invites the parent and child to find the best educational form that is possible at any given time, whether it is homeschooling, Montessori, Waldorf, Reggio Emilia, free school, democratic school, or public or independent school.

- Adolescence, the third era, is a time of both challenge and opportunity. The challenge requires parents to do all they can to stay in contact with their teen. The scope of opportunity is unknowable in advance. We know that adolescents have much greater capacity for creativity and contribution than we have allowed them so far in our culture. The parent's obligation and opportunity is once again to follow the child—this time, the adolescent—and provide support and nurturance as such may be helpful.

All of the young adults who speak in this book view the parenting they received as directly generative in relation to their own unfoldment so far in their lives, to their own becoming who they are at this moment when we meet them.

- Each one of them has access to post-modern consciousness, and several are accessing integral consciousness.

- Each has a clear sense that their life is a path that has meaning, that has purpose—and part or most of that purpose involves creative contribution and service.

- Each has an awareness of living in a unique moment in the history of our species in which global communication and travel are both easily accessible—and each has an identity that includes not only family and nation but also a global, planetary consciousness.

- Almost all of these young adults note that some significant element in their lives is a connection with soul or spirit.

All of these parents whom you have met in this book feel that they have succeeded in parenting "their young adults" in meaningful accord with their espoused values. And the young adults clearly agree. Their parents were imperfect but overwhelmingly effective. These young adults are deeply ethical, very much aware of themselves and others, and capable of complex and elegant metacognition. They also possess a sense of personal responsibility for the world they live in—not an immobilizing or guilt-laden sense but an empowering and directing sense.

These are all qualities of being that our evolution as a species requires. As Robert Gilman described it: "Assisting in the blossoming of this flower that already knows what it looks like when it blooms."

The greatest benefit of evolutionary parenting accrues to the persons who receive this gift of consciousness and love.

The second greatest gift goes to the parents, who can see the results of their efforts and whose lives are enriched by their continued connection with their child(ren).

The ultimate gift is to humanity—and to all life on our planet Earth.

David Marshak

APPENDIX ONE

Three Teachers of the Evolution Of Consciousness

Rudolf Steiner

When Rudolf Steiner died in 1924, he was a teacher and speaker known widely throughout western Europe. In the decades since his death, Steiner's contributions to our culture have not been eclipsed by the passage of time but, rather, have slowly gained a wider audience. His work has endured and may be more influential now than at any other time since his death.

Rudolf Steiner helped to invent and define eurythmy, a form of artistic movement that integrates spoken poetry and dance. He articulated a practice of bio-dynamic gardening, a sustainable method of agriculture based on harmony with the natural systems and cycles of the biosphere rather than an attempt to gain techno-logical domination over them. He organized the Anthroposophical Society, which continues as a center for spiritual study in western Europe, the United States, Australia, New Zealand, South Africa, and Brazil. He wrote about architecture, particularly the relation-ship between the structures people build and the lives they lead within them, and designed buildings that incorporated both sacred and secular space.

Steiner's most important contribution probably lies in the field of human development and education. For fifteen years Rudolf Steiner wrote and lectured about his vision of human becoming, particularly from birth through age twenty-one. He articulated a theory that is both profound and complex, that anticipated and still incorporates the work of developmental psychologists, such as Piaget and Erikson, and that extends into realms of human experience beyond cognitive and ego psychologies.

Steiner also articulated a theory and practice of education based on his vision of human becoming. In 1919 he founded a school, and he organized and supervised it until his death five years later. This school, called the Waldorf School because it originally served the children of employees in the Waldorf-Astoria cigarette factory in Stuttgart, Germany, provided the vehicle through which Steiner translated his educational theory into practice. It also became the model for what has grown into a worldwide network of several hundred Waldorf schools as well as a number of teacher training institutes.

Rudolf Steiner was born in 1861 in a small town on the border of Austria and Hungary. He studied mathematics and science at the Technical College in Vienna and, in 1891, received his doctorate from Rostock University. As a result of his work as a student, he was invited to serve as the editor of a portion of Goethe's scientific works. Although Steiner devoted much energy to this project both before and after earning his doctorate, he also wrote and published his own philosophical works and served as a teacher for many years.

From the age of seven, Steiner had experienced supersensible or spiritual realities beyond the material world as concrete and real. In his youth and early adulthood, he explored these planes and learned about their nature and meanings. By 1900 he had gained a good deal of control over his presence in these supersensible or spiritual realities. In that year Steiner first lectured publicly about his knowledge of supersensible realities, often focusing on the need for scientific research into the nature of these soul-spiritual planes. His lectures were well received, and he began to attract a following that viewed him as an enlightened spiritual teacher.

During his first decade of lecturing, Steiner was connected with the larger Theosophical movement of the time, which had a presence not only in western Europe but also in North America and India. From 1902 to 1912 Steiner headed the German section of the Theosophical Society and was an important voice within that movement. However, during the later years of this period, his disagreements with English leaders of the Society, particularly Annie Besant, led to a growing estrangement between him and the Theosophical movement. In 1913 Steiner broke with that movement and began to call his work not Theosophy but Anthroposophy, from the Greek *anthropos*, meaning man, and *sophia*, meaning wisdom. He also formed the Anthroposophical Society, centered in Dornach, near Basle, Switzerland.

Throughout the remaining decade of his life, Steiner continued to study supersensible realities through what he called "the science of the spirit" and to lecture about his learning. He attracted thousands of interested listeners as well as many who were hostile and violent toward his ideas. Despite increasing ill health, Steiner continued to give lectures and direct the original Waldorf School nearly to the time of his death.

Aurobindo Ghose

The life of Aurobindo Ghose was marked by stunning reversals and seeming contradictions. Yet, when viewed as a whole, the course of his life was consistent and clear. Aurobindo was born in India into an upper-caste Hindu family but spent most of his childhood and youth studying in England. He was a leader in the movement for Indian independence for four years before he suddenly abandoned politics and gave himself entirely to a spiritual life. Aurobindo devoted much of his time to meditation and yoga for the last four decades of his life and never left his ashram in southern India. Yet he wrote with clarity and insight about modern European and American science, politics, religion, psychology, and education as well as about his own spiritual knowledge and his understanding of Indian culture, history, and needs.

Rabindranath Tagore, the national poet of India and a Nobel laureate, wrote of Aurobindo after meeting him for the first time in 1928:

> I could realise he had been seeking for the soul and had gained it, and through this long process of realisation had accumulated

within him a silent power of inspiration. I felt that the utterance of the ancient Hindu Rishi spoke from him of that equanimity which gives the human soul its freedom and entrance into the all . . . I said to him: 'You have the Word and we are waiting to accept it from you. India will speak through your voice to the world.'[1]

While Aurobindo was revered by many in his native land, the recognition of his wisdom and gifts stretched far beyond the borders of India. Romain Rolland, the French man of letters and Nobel laureate, described Aurobindo as ". . . one of the greatest thinkers of modern India, [who] has realised the most complete synthesis between the genius of the East and the West."[2] Pitrim Sorokin, the Harvard sociologist, explained that "Sri Aurobindo's *The Life Divine* and other Yoga treatises are among the most important works of our time in philosophy, ethics, and humanities. Sri Aurobindo himself is one of the greatest living sages of our time; the most eminent moral leader."[3] And U Thant, the third Secretary General of the United Nations, called Aurobindo "one of the greatest spiritual leaders of all time."[4]

Aurobindo Ghose was born in Calcutta, India, in 1872. His father, an upper-caste member who had received his medical training in England, both despaired of the decadence and degradation of colonial India and admired the energy and power of Victorian English culture. In 1879 he sent all three of his sons to England for their schooling. Aurobindo, the youngest child, lived first with the family of an Anglican minister, then entered boarding school, and completed his studies at Cambridge University. Although his father had instructed that his sons be taught nothing about their native land, in his late teens Aurobindo learned of the incipient movement for the liberation of India from the British empire and became involved in student groups that agitated for Indian independence.

Aurobindo returned to India soon after his graduation in 1893. When he first stepped onto Indian soil, he discovered within himself a deep, unshakable feeling of inner peace. He later described this experience as the first step in his spiritual awakening. Aurobindo gained employment in Baroda, first as a civil servant and later as a teacher and vice-principal at Baroda College. In the decade after his return to his homeland, he devoted himself to studying the languages and cultures of India. He also began a secret involvement in the movement for Indian independence.

In 1906 Aurobindo moved to Calcutta to become principal of the Bengal National College. Here his previously secret commitment to political work soon became public, as he began to provide leadership for the independence movement in Bengal. Aurobindo edited a newspaper that promoted independence, spoke publicly about the need for passive resistance to British rule, and participated in the organization of a secret revolutionary group that began to prepare for the possibility of armed rebellion in the future. Within a year Aurobindo had become one of the major leaders of the nationalistic forces throughout Bengal.

In 1908 the British colonial authorities arrested Aurobindo, charged him with treason, and imprisoned him in Alipore jail. Aurobindo spent an entire year in prison awaiting his trial. In this time he studied the *Bhagavad Gita* and the *Upanishads* and intensified his yoga and meditation practice. In 1909 he was tried and acquitted. Immediately after his release, Aurobindo returned to his political work, speaking widely and starting two newspapers.

Within a few months, however, Aurobindo received what he felt to be a divine command to abandon his political work and take up an entirely spiritual life. At once he left Calcutta and traveled to Chandernagore in French India. A short time later he moved on to Pondicherry, a hundred miles south of Madras on the eastern coast of India, where he remained for the last forty years of his life. Despite the urging of his former political associates on many occasions, Aurobindo took no direct part in the independence movement after 1910.

Aurobindo had begun his practice of yoga in 1904. He had searched for a guru for several years but, finding none, had taught himself through his study of the ancient Hindu scriptures. In 1907, with the assistance of Sri Lele, Aurobindo experienced his first of four major spiritual openings: *samadhi*, the experience of oneness between self and Brahman, the ultimate reality.

Prior to his imprisonment in 1908, Aurobindo's yogic discipline had focused on his work for the independence of India. While in prison, Aurobindo devoted most of his time to spiritual practice and study, and his sense of mission broadened from India's liberation to that of the entire planet. While in Alipore jail he experienced his second spiritual opening: a vision of Krishna as a living, personal God who brought a transformation of light to all who surrendered themselves to Him.

When Aurobindo received his message to abandon his political work, he realized both that armed revolt would not be needed to free India from British rule and that his own calling was no longer Indian independence but the larger, more profound work of teaching humanity about the next step in its evolution. Within hours of receiving this message, Aurobindo let go of the life he had known for more than a decade and traveled to Chandernagore. Here he experienced his third illumination:

> . . . a vision of the supreme Reality as a multiform Unity, simultaneously static and dynamic, characterized by silence and expression, emptiness and creativity, infinite and yet composed of manifold forms.[5]

In this vision Aurobindo saw the Divine as both immanent in all things of the world and simultaneously transcendent to the world that humans know. He discovered the evolutionary need not to reject any part of reality, as many previous Hindu mystics had done, but to understand all of reality as divine and worthy of liberation.

In his first decade in Pondicherry, Aurobindo lived with a small group of followers who had come with him from Calcutta. From 1914 to 1921 he edited *Arya*, a journal in which he published in the form of serial articles most of what would constitute his major writings, including *The Life Divine, The Human Cycle, The Ideal of Human Unity*, and *Bases of Yoga*.

In 1914 Paul and Mira Richard (also known as Mira Alfassa, her maiden name), an upper-class French couple who were traveling in Asia in search of a spiritual teacher, had visited Aurobindo in Pondicherry. Both recognized him immediately as their guru. Paul had stayed on and helped to found *Arya* before returning to France to fight in World War I. Mira continued on her journey to Japan but returned to Pondicherry in 1920 to join Aurobindo as his student. Soon afterward he recognized her as The Mother, his own spiritual partner. He explained, "The Mother's consciousness is the divine consciousness. There is no difference between The Mother's path and mine; we have and have always had the same path."[6]

By 1926 Aurobindo's community of followers and students had grown from a handful of people to several hundred members. In that year Aurobindo experienced his fourth illumination: his "Day of Siddhi" when he felt the Overmind, a higher spiritual level of being than mind, descend into the physical plane of this planet. Immediately after this experience, Aurobindo turned over the responsibilities of administering this community, which soon took the form of the Sri Aurobindo Ashram, to Mira Richard. He retired into an almost complete seclusion for the rest of his life, although he stayed very much in touch with the world through periodicals and letters and did appear in public on four occasions each year. He also kept up a voluminous correspondence with his disciples in the ashram.

While Aurobindo lived in seclusion for the final third of his life, he broke his silence on two occasions. During World War II he saw Hitler and the Nazi forces as the expression of pure evil in the world and appealed to all Indians to put aside their grievances with the British temporarily and to support them in the war against Germany. In 1947 India received her independence on August 15, Aurobindo's seventy-fifth birthday, and Aurobindo delivered a radio speech about the significance of the day and the event.

Aurobindo Ghose died in 1950. Mira Richard lived on until 1973. In those twenty-three years she guided the Ashram and its attempt to embody Aurobindo's teachings. By the late 1960s the community had grown to more than two thousand members from all over the world. In 1968 the followers of Aurobindo founded Auroville, a spiritually based "city of the future" near the Ashram, which has been recognized by the Indian government as an international city-state.

Inayat Khan

The story of Inayat Khan's life is stranger and more surprising than any fiction of a holy man bringing a mystical tradition from the East. Inayat Khan grew up in a Muslim family, yet he also was much influenced by Hinduism. All of the men in his family were traditional Indian musicians. By his twentieth birthday Inayat was playing the veena, an Indian stringed instrument, for the court gatherings of rajahs and maharajahs throughout India. Later, for four years, he was the disciple of a Sufi master who, on his deathbed, sent Inayat to the United States to bring Sufism to the West. With his cousin and brothers, Inayat played traditional Indian music to accompany the performances of famous "Oriental dancers," like Mata Hari and Ruth St. Denis, in both the United States and in Europe, all the while teaching of the Sufi path and gaining disciples. Inayat Khan devoted the last third of his life to traveling throughout Europe and the United States, lecturing, delivering radio addresses, and teaching those who sought him out.

In his sixteen years in the West, Inayat Khan, called Hazrat[7] by his students, brought the teachings and practices of Sufism into the lives of thousands of westerners. He inspired and directed the organization of an international Sufi movement and the inception of Sufi communities in many cities in western Europe and the United States, some of which have endured to this day. His teachings, gathered in the volumes of *The Sufi Message of Hazrat Inayat Khan*, offer a rich and complex, mystically based vision of human nature and human becoming.

Inayat Khan was born in Baroda, India, in 1882. His family was Muslim in its origins. His grandfather, the central figure in the extended household of three generations, was Maula Bakhsh, a musician of wide repute who was known as the "Beethoven of India." Inayat's grandfather and father both held tolerant views about religious differences and were influenced by Hinduism as well as Islam. All of the grandchildren in the house attended Hindu schools and interacted with Hindu children as equals.

As a child Inayat learned to play the veena. In his middle teens he began to teach at the Academy of Music in Baroda, soon becoming a professor. He sought to educate people about the musical culture of India, to help them see traditional Indian music not just as Hindu or Muslim music but as a rich synthesis of both cultures.

In his late teens Inayat traveled across India playing sacred music in the courts of regional rulers. He also gave talks about music and culture. Although he was favorably received by rajahs and maharajahs and offered rich rewards, Inayat Khan felt his efforts to be largely a failure because most people in the ruling classes experienced his music not as the religious inspiration he intended but only as entertainment. He felt despair because he saw this limited appreciation as a degradation of Indian culture.

For a number of years around the turn of the century, Inayat had experienced visions that he did not understand. Eventually, he felt called to seek a spiritual teacher. After a search of several long and often frustrating years, in 1903 he found Murshid Syed Mohammed Abu Hashim Madani, a Sufi holy man. Inayat spent four years as Murshid Madani's disciple, during which time he began the spiritual practice he continued throughout his life. In 1907, only a few hours before his death, Murshid Madani gave Inayat his final instruction. He told the younger man, "Go to the Western world, my son, and unite East and West through the magic of your music. God has given you great capacities, and a great task to fulfill."[8]

In the next few years Inayat continued to travel throughout India, giving concerts and talks. On one tour he went on to Ceylon, Burma, and what was then called Cochin China: Laos, Cambodia, and Vietnam. Finally in 1910 he felt ready to heed his late master's instruction, and he sailed to New York City with his brother, Maheboob, and his cousin, Mohammed Ali. A year later his youngest brother, Musharaff, joined them. For two years they alternated between living in New York for months at a time and journeying across the North American continent on performance tours for equally long periods. Sometimes they played a concert of Indian music accompanied by a talk about Sufism by Inayat. More often they accompanied "Oriental dancers" like Ruth St. Denis who could attract the audience that they alone could not draw. Yet even in those often unruly crowds, some individuals could sense a holy power in Inayat and would seek him out later as a teacher. In 1911 Inayat initiated his first American disciple into the path of the Sufis.

Inayat Khan and his family traveled to London in 1912 and then on to Paris, playing music for the dance performances of the infamous Mata Hari but also giving talks and attracting students. In this year Inayat married Ora Ray Baker, a young American woman who had followed him to Europe, and in 1914, their first child was born. They would eventually have two girls and two boys. Yet even as he became the head of a family, Inayat continued to travel and teach in many European countries, including Germany and Russia.

In these years Inayat struggled with adapting the traditional Sufi teachings into a form that Westerners could understand and experience. "He was not propagating a new religion, he assured them—but an ancient Wisdom which threw a light on every religion of the world. This embraced the eternal truths common to all great teachings whether Hindu, Buddhist, Zoroastrian, Jewish, Christian, Muslim, or some other."[9] He sought to help people see how all of the world's religions shared a common center. This commonality focused on the knowledge that there is only one God in the universe of which all the gods are partial manifestations, and that there is only one human religion and one fundamental religious law: do unto others as you would have them do unto you. As he taught, Inayat asked people not to abandon their previous religious identity but to expand its meaning, so they could see its oneness with all other religions. His aim in his teaching, he explained, was ". . . to spread the wisdom of the Sufis which hitherto was a hidden treasure . . ."[10] and make the experience of God-realization available to everyone.

For several years, Inayat resisted both giving a name to his teachings and starting an organization to promote them. Yet gradually he recognized the need for both. He called his way the Sufi path, a term derived from *safa*, meaning purified of ignorance and egotism. He explained that Sufism was not in essence an element of Islam but, rather, a much older mystical tradition that predated

Judaism and Hinduism and that had found expression in every major world religion. In 1915 Inayat reluctantly founded the first Sufi organization, the Sufi Movement. Later he organized the Sufi Order, an inner school of mysticism for initiates.

Inayat Khan and his family spent the years of World War I in England. Inayat had written his first book—in English—in 1913, and he devoted a good part of his energy to other writing projects. His musical performances, which had become more and more infrequent, ended altogether by 1915, and the remainder of his time was devoted to teaching initiates.

Once the war had ended, Inayat began the last phase of his life during which he devoted most of each year to traveling throughout the nations of Europe, lecturing and establishing Sufi centers. He moved to France in 1920 and then on to Geneva, Switzerland, three years later, where he established the headquarters of the Sufi Movement. He journeyed repeatedly through Belgium, Holland, Italy, and the Scandinavian countries, always giving talks and teaching initiates. In 1923 and again in 1925 he toured the United States.

In 1926 Inayat Khan returned to India for the first time in sixteen years. He visited many shrines and holy places. Although he was only forty-four years old as the new year began, his picture shows the aged face of a man who seems at least two decades older. Inayat's exhaustive pace had worn down his body and sickened him several times during the previous six years. Each time he had aged noticeably, yet he had recovered. In February 1927 while still in India, Inayat Khan became ill again, this time with pneumonia. Within a few days, he was dead.

Notes

1. Langley, *Sri Aurobindo: Indian Poet, Philosopher, and Mystic*, 13.
2. Motwani, *Three Great Sages*, 24–25.
3. Mitra, *Sri Aurobindo and the New World*, 49.
4. Gandhi, *Contemporary Relevance of Sri Aurobindo*, 327.
5. Bruteau, *Worthy Is the World: The Hindu Philosophy of Sri Aurobindo*,   31.
6. Ghose, *Sri Aurobindo on Himself and The Mother*, 6.
7. *Hazrat* is a reverent form of address in the Sufi tradition, meaning saint. Its use by Inayat Khan's disciples conveys their perception of him not as an avatar, like Buddha or Jesus, the most holy of human forms, but as a great initiate who helps to bring disciples to an understanding of and feeling for the teachings of the avatars.
8. Van Stolk, *Memories of a Sufi Sage, Hazrat Inayat Khan*, 27.
9. Ibid., 28.
10. Khan, *The Sufi Message of Hazrat Inayat Khan: VIII*, 135.

APPENDIX TWO

Why Maria Montessori Is Omitted

There are so many striking similarities between the common vision of Steiner, Aurobindo, and Inayat Khan and the teachings of Maria Montessori that I can only conclude that all four of these teachers were drawing on the same apprehension of reality and truth. Indeed Montessori even publicized her vision at the very same time as her three "colleagues." Her first training course for teachers in Italy began in 1909, to be followed by publication of her various books and articles during the next decade. Her first international training course began in 1913. Yet by the late 1920s Montessori was no longer engaged in the research of new perspectives and methods. Rather she devoted her efforts to the preservation of the existing Montessori movement. So, as with her "colleagues," Montessori's period of discovery came to a close before the end of the 1920s.

Some of the most important ways in which Montessori's vision is identical with or similar to Steiner's, Aurobindo's, and Inayat Khan's common vision are these:

Montessori described the newborn child as a "spiritual embryo" and understood the child's nature as a whole system, including the sub-systems of vital energy (what she called *horme*), physical body, and mind. She described these sub-systems as interrelated and interpenetrated.

Montessori taught that each child contains vital energy or horme that directs her growth by motivating her to meet her growth needs during each period of development. This vital energy serves as an inner guide for the child. Parents and teachers must give the child freedom to follow her inner guide. When the child can do so, she develops both her will and her concentration.

Montessori defined three periods of development in the life of the child and youth: from birth through age 6; from 6 to 12 years; and from 12 to 18 years. (She also defined a fourth period at the end of adolescence, from 18 to 24 years.) Each period contains *sensitive periods*: times at which the child is developmentally ready for a particular kind of growth and must accomplish this growth if she is to develop to her potential.

Montessori maintained that the will of the child must be nurtured, and never broken.

Montessori described the child's primary means of learning during the first period of growth as her "absorbent mind." Absorption and imitation are two ways to describe the same process of learning.

Montessori taught that the function of education is to give the child opportunities to express her inner guide within an appropriately prepared and safe learning environment. An education based on this principle will help the child to develop independence, self-discipline, concentration, motivation, and sensitivity.

Finally, Montessori taught that the role of the teacher is not to control or direct the child but rather to prepare the learning environment and then nurture and support the child. For this work, the teacher must focus on the development of her own spirit, character, and imagination. She must understand that her work is to be of service to the child's spirit and that the child will reveal who she is becoming over time.

All of these significant understandings of Maria Montessori

are identical with or similar to those of the common vision of Steiner, Aurobindo, and Inayat Khan. And, of course, I would be the first to agree that there is much more in common between Montessori and her three "colleagues" than between Montessori and more traditional educational models. Why then have I not included her as an author of what I call the common vision? I have made this judgment for the following reasons:

Although she calls the child a "spiritual embryo" and employs some of the language of the spirit, Montessori's vision does not describe or detail the spiritual elements of human beings. Thus, it omits significant aspects both of the description of human beings as whole systems that include spiritual energies and of the spiritual context in which we live.

Although Montessori's vision does deal with some issues of the emotions, it does not provide a systemic exploration of the sub-system of the vital being. Thus, her vision does not deal in a comprehensive way with the whole realm of the emotions, desires, and feelings, an important set of elements in describing human unfoldment and in articulating principles and practices for child raising and education.

Montessori's vision does explore the relationship between the physical body and the mind as the child grows. However, it does not contain the richness of description of the interrelationships among the physical, vital, mental, and spiritual sub-systems of the child and youth that is offered in the common vision of Inayat Khan, Steiner, and Aurobindo.

Finally, Montessori urges that the child be encouraged to develop her cognition during the second half of the first era of unfoldment. She argues that these years are a sensitive period for the development of writing skills and for the learning of vocabulary, grammar, and numbers. While, of course, she would not teach any of this directly, she prepares the learning environment in such a way that the materials there encourage the child to embark on this kind of learning. Steiner, Aurobindo, and Inayat Khan strongly disagree with this approach. While they note that the child can learn all of this effectively during these years, they maintain that it is profoundly undesirable for such topics and skills to become the focus of learning. Rather, these years should be a time of imaginative, self-directed, noncompetitive play. Such play helps the child to develop her spiritual nature in its fullness and to prepare for her transition from the first era into the second.

Maria Montessori's teachings are clearly a visionary work of genius. So I mean no disrespect for Montessori by omitting her from authorship of what I call the common vision. Obviously she articulated significant sections of this common vision in her work. Yet I have chosen not to include her (1) because she does not provide significant sections of this vision, none of which are left out by Steiner, Aurobindo, or Inayat Khan, and (2) because she characterizes the needs of the second part of the first era of childhood in a profoundly divergent way from her colleagues.

So far Montessori's work has had a much greater impact on the world of schools than that of all three of her colleagues together. So clearly Maria Montessori has made a profound contribution to the evolution of human consciousness on this planet.

ABOUT THE AUTHOR

David Marshak lives in Bellingham, Washington. He is also the author of *The Common Vision: Parenting and Educating for Wholeness.*

David is the founding president of the SelfDesign Graduate Institute. SelfDesign is a contemporary expression of the *common vision.*

Made in the USA
San Bernardino, CA
26 March 2018